The Leadership Skills Handbook

Fourth edition

The Leadership Skills Handbook

90 essential skills you need to be a leader

Jo Owen

KoganPage

First published in Great Britain and the United States in 2006 by Kogan Page Limited
Fourth edition published 2017

2nd Floor, 45 Gee Street	c/o Martin P Hill Consulting	4737/23 Ansari Road
London	122 W 27th St, 10th Floor	Daryaganj
EC1V 3RS	New York, NY 10001	New Delhi 110002
United Kingdom	USA	India

www.koganpage.com

© Jo Owen, 2017

The right of Jo Owen to be identified as the author of this work has been asserted by him in accordance with the Copyright, Designs and Patents Act 1988.

ISBN   978 0 7494 8033 2
E-ISBN   978 0 7494 8034 9

British Library Cataloguing-in-Publication Data

A CIP record for this book is available from the British Library.

Library of Congress Cataloging-in-Publication Data

Names: Owen, Jo, author.
Title: The leadership skills handbook : 90 essential skills you need to be a
    leader / Jo Owen.
Description: 4th Edition. | New York : Kogan Page Ltd, [2017] | Revised
    edition of the author's The leadership skills handbook, 2014.
Identifiers: LCCN 2017022500 (print) | LCCN 2017027707 (ebook) | ISBN
    9780749480349 (ebook) | ISBN 9780749480332 (pbk.) | ISBN 9780749480349
    (eISBN)
Subjects: LCSH: Leadership–Handbooks, manuals, etc. | Management–Handbooks,
    manuals, etc.
Classification: LCC HD57.7 (ebook) | LCC HD57.7 .O947 2017 (print) | DDC
    658.4/092–dc23
LC record available at https://lccn.loc.gov/2017022500

Typeset by Integra Software Services, Pondicherry
Print production managed by Jellyfish
Printed and bound by CPI Group (UK) Ltd, Croydon CR0 4YY

CONTENTS

ACKNOWLEDGEMENTS

This book reflects the collective knowledge, wisdom and experience of thousands of leaders who have contributed through surveys, interviews and real experience. I am especially grateful to the outstanding leaders of the future at Teach First who have effectively tested and challenged many of the ideas in this book. Our future is in good hands when they do emerge as our leaders.

I would not have written the book without the encouragement of Helen Kogan at Kogan Page. Professor Nigel Nicholson at London Business School generously gave time, insight and hospitality, and Dr Nick Baylis at Cambridge University has opened up whole new vistas on leadership through his positive psychology work.

The faults in this book are all mine. I could not have wished for better support and insight from such a wonderful group of people.

I would like to thank those many organizations for which I have worked across the world. There is no substitute for seeing leadership in action: it is never as simple as it looks in books. So my thanks go to:

ABN Amro
Accenture
Achievement for All
AEGON
Airbus
ALICO
American Express
Apple Computers
Armstrong Industries
Aviva
Barclays Bank
BT
Cap Gemini

Central Bank of Indonesia
Chase Group
Citigroup
Crown Prosecution Service
Edexcel
EDS
Future Leaders
Gemini
Google
Hallmark Cards
HBOS
HCA
IBM

ItoChu
Lloyds Bank
Merrill Lynch
MetLife
Mitsubishi Chemicals
Monsanto
National Air Traffic
    Services
NCB
NHS
Nordea Bank
Norwegian Dairy
    Association
Philips
Procter & Gamble
Qualcomm
RBS
Rentokil

RHM
Royal Sun Alliance
SABIC
San Miguel
SDP
Skype
Symantec
Start Up
STIR
SWIFT
Symantec
Teach First
Teaching Leaders
Thorn Rental
UBS
Unilever
Union Carbide
Zurich Financial Services

Introduction

Most leadership books try to answer the question, 'What is good leadership?' That is like trying to answer the question, 'What are people like?' The resulting debate generates more heat than light because leaders, like people, come in many different shapes and sizes.

This handbook is different. It starts with the question, 'How can you learn to lead?' In our research with over 1,000 leaders at all levels in public, private and voluntary sectors the answer was clear: leaders learn not from courses but from experience, bosses, peers and role models. Some of the lessons are positive: we try to copy effective behaviour. Some lessons are negative: we see a boss or peer explode spectacularly and quietly decide not to copy that mistake.

The problem with learning from experience is that it is a random walk. Bump into good role models and experiences and you learn good lessons. Get the wrong role models and experience and you learn the wrong lessons. Not many people become leaders through the luck of the random walk. This handbook will help you take the randomness out of the random walk of experience. It gives you a framework for observing and learning from the experiences you go through. The structure takes some of the randomness out of random experience and lets you learn faster and better than your peers: this is your guide to accelerated leadership.

Our research identified the main practical skills that leaders must have. No leader gets ticks in all the boxes. But you need to develop some signature strengths – and you do not want to fail badly in any area.

The book does not prescribe a single formula for success. You will not have to become Nelson Mandela, Genghis Khan or Mother Teresa to succeed. The book allows you to create your own formula for success. Your success formula will reflect a combination of what works in your sector, organization and profession plus what works for you as an individual.

The leadership riddle

There are two dead-end roads to leadership. The first is to try to be someone else. We cannot be Churchill, Gandhi and Alexander the Great all rolled into one (although there are some people who think they are already that good). We have to be true to ourselves. The other dead end is to simply be who we are, in the vain hope that the world will recognize our innate brilliance and leadership talent. We could end up waiting a very long time.

So now we have a problem: we cannot become leaders by being someone else, and we cannot succeed by being who we are. How do we solve this riddle? The solution is that we have to become the best of who we are. This book is your guide to discovering how to do so. It will help you discover, build and celebrate your strengths. You will not have to sacrifice your personality: you can be a leader on your own terms, not on the terms of some guru with a great theory.

This handbook helps you take the randomness out of the journey to leadership. The book features the core skills leaders need to develop. Each skill has a framework to help you think about how that skill should be deployed ideally. As important, note and learn from your own experience examples of where you see the skill being deployed well or less well. You should think hard about why it was effective or less effective. As you observe and record real-life examples of skills in action, you will be developing your own unique formula for success in your own unique context.

This handbook is to be used by you to create your own leadership DNA. Ideal leadership is always inferior to practical leadership: what works for you where you are. The handbook only succeeds if you use it as an active tool. When you are faced with an unfamiliar challenge, refer back to this handbook and your notes. Use the book well and it can become your personal guide and coach on the road to leadership.

The CMI (Chartered Management Institute) kindly voted this book as its Book of the Year for New Managers in 2013. It is as a result of this vote of confidence that I have continued this project to help new managers become better managers faster. This new edition has been expanded to include completely new sections on managing the art of politics and influence within the firm, and it also includes new sections on mastering the basics of finance and strategy. It is now your comprehensive resource for the skills you need to become a successful leader.

Finally, it is worth learning one lesson from the world's top athletes. Each gold medallist is supreme in one discipline: they focus relentlessly on becoming the best at one thing. They do not focus on their weaknesses. No one asks weightlifters to improve their synchronized swimming skills. Leaders, like athletes, cannot succeed at everything. They have to focus on their strengths, practise relentlessly and find the context or discipline in which they can flourish. As a manager, you have some unique talents. Focus on what you are great at, and find the context in which your talents will flourish.

Part One
Mindset skills

01
Positive leadership

Cynicism is in plentiful supply in the lower reaches of many organizations. There are many cynical junior and middle managers who are going to stay that way: cynical and junior. Our research found no effective leaders who were cynical about their work, their organization, themselves or their lives. They were relentlessly positive about everything.

Being positive is different from the hippy mantra of 'Be happy; don't worry.' Positive leadership is a frame of mind where leaders:

- look to the future, not to the past;
- focus on action, not on analysis;
- see possibilities, not just problems;
- take control versus being controlled;
- create options versus accepting the status quo.

Some people behave like this naturally. For the rest of us, the good news is that these are habits that can be learnt. Choose which set of questions from Table 1.1 you want, in a tough situation, to be working on in your head. Keep asking yourself these questions and you will run a serious risk of appearing and acting like a positive and effective leader.

Table 1.1   Asking the right questions

Leader mindset	Follower mindset
What are some possible solutions/options/ways forward?	What went wrong?
What can I do now to regain control and build momentum?	Why have I been put in this position?
Whose support do I need and how will I get it?	Who messed up? Who is going to put this right?
What can I learn from this?	How do I avoid the blame?

In our research, we came across some outstanding examples of leaders thinking positively:

- An arsonist had burned down one wing of the school. The head-teacher saw this as a great opportunity to redesign and rebuild the school in the way she wanted it to be, and the insurance company would pay. She was not, as far as we know, responsible for the arson attack.

- The Japanese subsidiary of a multinational was losing US $2 million a year and jobs were at risk. The leader of the subsidiary persuaded head office that it should invest US $2 million a year in building its Japanese subsidiary. Head office thought this was great. Losses (bad) were miraculously converted into investment (good) and everyone was happy.

- The politician was meeting voters, and always wanted to say something nice to them. One person came up and introduced himself as a pawnbroker: what can you say that is positive about that? 'Wonderful... pawnbroking is where banking really started hundreds of years ago... and you are still the only people who provide banking services to the poor. You provide a very important and historic service.' One more vote in the bag as the pawnbroker disappeared, happy, down the street.

> Cynical junior and middle managers are going to stay that way: cynical and junior.

02
Responsibility

Responsibility is massively abused in management speak. Most people's hearts sink when responsibility comes into the conversation: it is rarely a positive development.

It can be used as a guilt trip by senior managers on team members: 'Remember you are responsible for the outcome of this project.' It can be used as petty politics to define and defend territory: 'This is my responsibility; if I need your help I will ask for it.' It can be used by jobsworths to avoid responsibility: 'I can't do that: it's not my responsibility. It's more than my job's worth to let you do that.'

So forget how the organization abuses the idea of responsibility, and focus on what it means for you as a leader. Here are three things that all leaders must be responsible for, and where many people struggle:

1 **You are responsible for your career.** If you have a lousy job with a lousy boss in a lousy organization, who is responsible for that? Only when you take responsibility for your own destiny can you start to control it. At times, your choices may be very uncomfortable, but you always have choices.

2 **You are responsible for what happens to you, even the bad stuff.** 'I got ripped off first for £500,000, then for £5 million and finally for £50 million within five years. So I was making progress, of sorts: the disasters were at least getting bigger and more interesting. At first I blamed the people who ripped me off. Then I realized that if I was a victim, then I was only a victim of my own folly in letting myself be ripped off.' Once you take responsibility, you take control and you start to make progress.

Until that point you are a victim of a cruel world: leaders never let themselves become victims. They take control.

3 **You are responsible for your own feelings.** This is the killer, literally. Research shows that pessimists die sooner and have a lower quality of life than optimists. And if you want to feel angry, frustrated and upset with your colleagues, that is your choice: there is no law that says you must. And if you feel that way, the chances are your feelings will affect your colleagues and things will only get worse. Or you can feel calm, positive and action-focused: your colleagues are likely to respond better. It takes time to retrain instinctive reactions and feelings, but it can be done. The starting point is to realize that how you feel is how you choose to feel: choose well.

All of this qualifies as a BFO: a Blinding Flash of the Obvious. But it is so obvious that it is very hard to see, especially in the heat of battle or in the slough of despond when emotions can overwhelm sense. As George Orwell wrote: 'To see what is in front of your nose requires a constant struggle.'

If you can see this and act on it, you will not only
lead better: you will live better and longer.

03
High aspirations

L ow aspirations are self-fulfilling. People who believe they can, and people who believe they can not, are both usually right.

You may think that people in senior positions lack talent or competence. The low aspiration response is to complain about them. The high aspiration response is to realize that you can do better than them: you should be able to join the leadership ranks. The great entrepreneurs of the world did not succeed by thinking small: they dared to think big and played to win.

High aspirations by themselves are just a pipe dream. We can all dream of becoming a top musician or sports star, or perhaps a billionaire. But dreaming is not enough. Every top sports star has a long history of obsessive training. High aspirations demand hard work. It can take 20 years to become an overnight success.

High aspirations should extend to everything you do. 'Good enough' is the motto for also-rans, especially in today's world where work is ambiguous and open-ended. High aspirations mean constant challenge: challenge yourself to do better, learn more and achieve excellence.

If you want a high-performing team, do not be afraid to set high expectations. Most people rise or fall to the level of expectations they encounter. By setting high expectations, you help your team achieve more and develop faster. Provided you support and help them, they will be grateful to be part of a high-performing team, not a 'B' team.

In practice, complacency is the enemy of high aspirations and high performance. In many organizations over 90 per cent of staff are rated as above average. This is statistically impossible, but emotionally inevitable: no one likes to be told they are below average. As a test, are you below or above average in terms of honesty, effort, competence, driving ability and love making? Few people care to rate themselves below average. But if we already think we are above average, we see little need to improve. We lack the objective performance data that drives sprinters and other athletes on to ever better performance.

To make aspirations a reality, you need to ask yourself a few simple questions:

- Where do I really want to be in five (or ten) years' time?
- Where do I think I will be in five (or ten) years' time given what I am doing now?
- What do I need to do differently (building skills, new roles and experiences) to achieve my goals?
- Am I prepared to do what it takes (time, effort, risk)?
- So what do I need to do differently now?

If you are satisfied with your performance, your aspirations are not high enough. We can all do better if we have the courage to challenge ourselves, test ourselves and learn and develop.

> People who believe they can and people who believe they cannot are both usually right.

04
Have courage

If you follow the herd, you will never get ahead of the herd. You can have a quiet and relatively safe career by following the herd. If you want to lead, you have to take some risk.

In any organization there are moments of truth where people shine or shrink. There are crises, where no one is sure what to do; there are new ideas and projects that need a champion to take the lead; and there are moments of uncertainty where direction is needed but lacking. These are all moments when leaders step up and followers step back.

Fortunately, courage is not something you are born with or without. You can learn courage. The chief of the fire service exploded with anger when it was suggested that his firemen must be very brave to go into burning buildings. 'I don't want brave firemen. Brave firemen become dead firemen fast!' So how does he get raw recruits to do things that most of us would consider brave and dangerous? First, he makes them learn how to deploy a ladder. Then he trains them to climb a few feet safely. Then he exposes them to a small fire in a bucket. And slowly the heights and the fires get bigger and bigger. Eventually, the recruits become fully trained firemen. They do things which seem courageous to us, but are routine to them.

As with firemen, so with managers. We can learn courage. Start with small steps. We are often braver away from work: use family experience and perhaps volunteering experience to learn how to hold your ground, to push new ideas and to take the lead. At work, volunteer for discretionary projects: they are a great chance to learn and develop. Learn to stand up for your interests; challenge nonsense when you see it rather than complaining about it later around the water cooler.

Courage is built one step at a time, which means taking no more than small risks to start with. Very brave managers are like very brave firemen: they risk a premature demise. Once you know how to take smaller risks, you can take the larger risks comfortably. When you are familiar with risks and know how to manage them, they cease to be risks.

- Where have you pushed yourself beyond your comfort zone in the last three months?
- What did you learn and how could you improve?
- Where do you want to push yourself in the next three months?

> If you follow the herd, you will never get ahead of the herd.

05
Be adaptable

Carbon dating is a good way of dating fossils. Music is a good way of dating the living fossils of management. Ask people what their favourite music and films are, and most people will date themselves pretty accurately: people who like The Doors and Dire Straits are older than those who like Coldplay and The Smiths, who are older than the fans of Rihanna. And if you still like the Spice Girls, just keep quiet about it.

The same is true of films, books and management. There is a time when we are learning, absorbing and changing and then... and then we are in danger of ossifying and becoming a fossil living in a time warp of our own. We have all come across old-time managers who use their malign experience to tell you that they have seen it all before: it didn't work then and it won't work now. But standing still in a fast-changing world is dangerous to your career.

Most managers learn a success formula early in their careers. They learn by seeing how their peers and bosses succeed or mess up, and they copy and avoid those examples as necessary. But the problem is that the success formula will not stay the same over your career. For instance, expectations change as you progress through an organization:

- Entry level: work hard, be reliable, learn your craft.
- Front line manager: delegate, motivate, monitor and develop staff.

- Middle manager: make things happen through people you do not control, influence, build alliances, work agendas, deal with ambiguity and conflicting goals.
- Top manager: strategic vision, excellent communications, deal with high-level external stakeholders, good financial sense.

As you progress you have to learn new functional skills: marketing people eventually have to understand finance and HR; IT people have to learn about customers and markets, and so on. To succeed, you have to keep learning, growing and developing. If you are still doing stock checks for the annual audit at the age of 50, you do not have the right skill set to be the partner in charge, even if your stock checks are brilliant. You can let your taste in music remain unchanged; you cannot afford to let your skills remain unchanged.

Test yourself

- What new skills have you developed in the last three years?
- What new skills will you need in the next stage of your career?
- Are you learning the skills you will need for the future?

06
Learn to be lucky

All successful leaders admit to being lucky: they create their own luck. The question is how to create your own luck. Try the 5P luck programme:

1 **Practice.** The more you practise, the luckier you get. The long-shot putt becomes a 50/50 putt; the 50/50 becomes easy. Practice converts luck into skill.

2 **Persistence.** The difference between failure and success is giving up. Setbacks are great learning experiences: most leaders and entrepreneurs have more than their share of setbacks.

3 **Preparation.** If you do not know what you are looking for, you will not find it. Know what you want; hunt it persistently.

4 **Positive outlook.** Look for solutions, not problems. Look for action, not analysis. Be confident in yourself: if you are not enthusiastic, no one else will be. Don't get sucked into a culture of negativity. All this means that luck can be learnt.

5 **Perspective.** We are as lucky as we feel. If you focus on all that goes wrong in the day, you will feel you have bad luck. If you count all your blessings, suddenly you will feel lucky. You are as lucky as you choose to be. Choose well.

Focus on luck

Review all the setbacks you have had. Are you lucky? Review all the successes and narrow escapes you have had. Are you still unlucky? Luck is largely a matter of self-perception.

Look at all the problems you have. Feeling bad? Look at all the options you have and how you might achieve them. Feeling better? Now find some practical first steps and move to action.

Look at some successful entrepreneurs. Aren't their ideas obvious? You or I could have done it as well. The entrepreneurs do not even look smart intellectually or socially. So I must be able to do better than them. Right now, someone is making the next obvious idea into a big success. Why shouldn't that person be you?

> Leaders create their own luck.

07
Managing stress

If you find it hard to get to sleep, you are not alone. There is a quiet epidemic of stress among managers and leaders, and it comes directly from the changed nature of work. In the past, work and leisure were compartmentalized. If business people had a brief-case, it was to carry their sandwiches and a newspaper. The shackles of e-mail and the internet did not exist. But now work and leisure are co-mingled: we do personal business at work and we work even at home.

To make matters worse, work has become ambiguous. It is never clear when your work as a leader is done. There is always some-thing more you can do. If you produce a report, it could be two pages or 200. And even if it is 200 pages, there is always another fact or opinion you could gather, another analysis you could do. And so even if we leave the office, the office never leaves us. There are armies of leaders thinking, not sleeping, each night.

There are several radical options for dealing with stress:

- Drop out and start your vegan farm.
- Become a Buddhist monk.
- See a shrink – or become one.

Most of us do not have the luxury of taking these options unless we want to lose our house and family. So we need something more practical. You have five ways of dealing with stress:

1 **Take control.** The difference between pressure and stress is control. If you are working very hard but you are in control, you may get tired but you will not get stressed. Now take away control: you are no longer in control of events on which your

future depends. Suddenly your stress levels will go through the roof. The trick is to focus on what you can control and influence: if you can do something about it, do it. If you cannot do anything, it is pointless worrying about it. Even if it is only a small thing, do it: give yourself the impression of control and hope. Don't worry about things you cannot control.

2 **Compartmentalize your life.** You do not have to answer e-mails in the middle of the night or on holiday. Create barriers and set expectations with colleagues appropriately. Even the godfather of time and motion, Frederick Taylor, found that regular breaks did not interrupt production: they improved productivity by making sure workers were refreshed for the work at hand. Compartmentalizing your life is easy if you have clear goals for the week and for each day: you will know when you have reached a reasonable milestone and you can start to switch off. If you have no clear goals, then by definition your work will never finish because you will never reach your goals.

3 **Get help.** The easiest way to get something done is to get someone else to do it for you. It's called delegation. Delegation is a great way to show trust in your team and to help them grow and develop. Do not try to do it all yourself: your team will not thank you for hogging all the interesting work. Find a coach; find friends or family you can talk to. A problem shared is a problem halved. Often the simple act of talking about a challenge resolves it.

4 **Find the right role.** Some roles are inherently more stressful than others, and many people enjoy such high-octane jobs: stress junkies need stressful roles. If you are not a stress junkie but you are in a role where stress is part of the job description, then you may want to think about whether you are in the right role.

5 **Keep perspective.** Over the years I have cancelled big family events for the sake of some urgent and important crisis at work. I now have no idea what those famous work battles were all about, but I still feel the pain of missing the family events. The sky will not fall down without you holding it up for the rest of humanity. Keep a clear sense of your priorities and act accordingly.

08
Honesty

For a leader, honesty is not just about morals and ethics; it is much more important than that. Honesty is about survival.

Who wants to work for you?

Think about the leaders you have wanted to work for, versus those you have had to work for. How many of the leaders you have wanted to work for did you not trust? The chances are, you trust the leaders you want to work for. And you probably only trust people who are honest with you.

If people have to follow you because of your power and position, they will. But do not be fooled into thinking they want to follow you unless they trust you. To build trust with your followers, you have to be honest with them. This is hard-form honesty: telling the whole truth promptly, even when it is painful. This is an honesty test most politicians fail; then they wonder why no one trusts them.

Authority and popularity are weak currencies for leadership. Authority can be removed in a reorganization. Popularity leads to weakness: you avoid the difficult conversations; you avoid stretching the team too far; you accept excuses. Honesty and trust are the true currencies for leadership. No one can take them away from you. Honesty and trust build respect, which lasts longer than popularity.

Honesty is tough

Someone is not meeting your expectations. Do you tell the person now or let it slide in the hope that things might get better anyway?

The business is facing difficulties. Do you tell the staff or keep quiet because bad news might unsettle them?

In each case, failing to act promptly simply builds up bigger problems for later, and failure to act is corrosive of the trust you need to build.

> Honesty is not just about morals and ethics. It's about survival.

09
Self-awareness

No leader gets ticks in all the boxes. This is deeply reassuring: you do not have to be perfect to lead. Look around you, and you will see that all leaders are flawed in some way. Having a weakness, or a 'development opportunity' in today's jargon, is not an obstacle to leadership if you know what to do about it.

Effective leaders are keenly aware of what they are good at and what they are not good at. It takes great self-confidence, self-awareness and humility to admit to not being good at things. But that is the critical first step towards doing something about it.

All leaders have weaknesses, but fortunately leadership is a team sport. The first act of a good leader should be to assemble a good team. An ineffective team will all be clones of the leader. An effective team will complement the leader's technical strengths and personal style. Your job is not to be the best person on the team. As a leader, your job is to get all the best people onto the team.

High self-awareness allows you to focus on your signature strengths. Just as we all have weaknesses, we all have strengths. The trick is to know what you are uniquely good at doing, and then do more of it. Deal with weaknesses by building a team and delegating: if you are lousy at tax management, find an accountant who can do that for you.

Self-awareness is also essential day to day. We have all been in meetings where someone drones on, completely unaware that he or she is boring or irritating everyone else; we have seen people lose the plot and lose their temper. The best leaders do not do this. They have an ability to detach and watch themselves from the outside. They become a fly on the wall, watching their own performance and asking some simple questions:

- If I was listening to this, how would I react?
- How are the others reacting?
- What do the people listening want and need to hear?

This is different from the internal dialogue inside inexperienced managers' heads:

- How can I get my point across?
- I wish they would shut up so I can make my point.
- Why don't these idiots understand I am right?

Highly self-aware managers are acutely aware of others and see themselves through the eyes of other people. Managers with low self-awareness only see their world through their own warped eyes.

> It takes great self-confidence, self-awareness and humility to admit to not being good at things.

Developing self-awareness

Make an honest (and humble) list of what you are good at and what you are not good at in terms of:

- technical skills;
- interpersonal and leadership skills;
- personal style.

Now have someone you know and trust review the list with you. You can do the same for the other person and make it a two-way exercise. Finally, review the strengths and weaknesses of your team: have you got the balance right?

> No leader gets ticks in all the boxes.

10
Working to win

Athletes, like leaders, do not win by playing to their weaknesses and imagining failure. They win by building on their strengths and rehearsing, visualizing success in their minds. Leaders have an advantage over athletes: leaders can delegate to other people to compensate for their own weaknesses. From this come four simple principles of working to win:

1 **Play to your strengths.** Know what you are good at and in what context (occupation, company and project).

2 **Visualize success.** This is important before big, stressful events. Walk through each step of the event, seeing what a successful outcome looks like, feels like, smells like and sounds like. Rehearse it as vividly as possible. Then make it happen.

3 **Think like a winner.** Remember all the times you have done great things. Let yourself get back into that frame of mind. When you believe you will succeed, you will. Failure is a self-fulfilling prophecy. If you have no enthusiasm or confidence, no one else will be enthusiastic or confident for you.

4 **Create a team that compensates for your weaknesses.** If you are no good at accounting, for instance, rest assured there are thousands of accountants out there to help.

Learning to work to win

Draw up your list of strengths and weaknesses. See what you can do to work in situations that play to your strengths, and start looking for people you can partner with to compensate for your weaknesses.

Try visualizing success and rehearsing as vividly as possible the sights, sounds, smells, feelings and actions of success. Visualize your biggest successes as vividly as possible. These successes define who you are. You are a winner, so keep winning.

Failure is a self-fulfilling prophecy. If you have no enthusiasm or confidence, no one else will be enthusiastic or confident for you.

Part Two
Career skills

01
Your leadership journey: key principles

Your potential is defined by your ambition and your ability (see Figure 2.1).

For a moment, we will assume that, since you have bought this book and taken the trouble to read this far, you are showing the sort of ambition required of a leader. People with low ambition are unlikely to read this book. So you can put yourself in the upper half of the diagram in Figure 2.1. We can, naturally, also assume that you are talented. The only real question is whether you are developing the right sort of talent to be an effective leader.

Schools teach exactly the wrong sorts of skills for becoming a leader. In school you are working by yourself to predetermined goals where there is an intellectually correct answer. Any aspiring leader who waits to be set goals, thinks all the answers are rational and works alone is unlikely to succeed. Leadership requires crafting an agenda (setting goals, not just accepting them), working in a deeply political world and working closely with other people. Schools do not teach this. Business school fails dismally to teach this. And most corporate training swings wildly between technical training (accounting and systems) and tree hugging, raft building and team building on the other side.

In reality, you cannot be taught to lead. You have to discover how to lead through experience and observation. To help you structure your leadership journey, look at Figure 2.2. This is your entire leadership career laid out before you.

Figure 2.1   Leadership success matrix

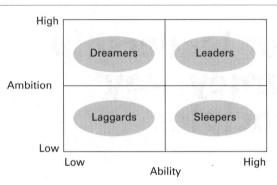

Figure 2.2   The Leader's skills and career

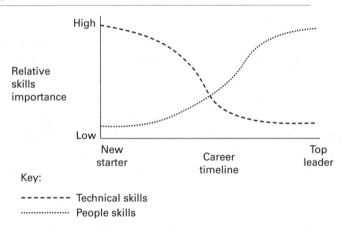

Most people start their careers learning some basic technical skills. This trade craft is unique to each trade: accounting, law, IT, financial analysis, psychology or dealing in the tripartite asset-collateralized repo market. You can make small fortunes through technical skills: Premiership footballers are highly skilled and highly paid, but they are not leaders.

Technical skills are a trap. Many people see promotion as an opportunity to deal with more complex technical problems and to solve those that beat other people. That is not leadership: leadership requires getting other people to do things, it is not about doing it all yourself. The CEO cannot solve every problem in the organization from unfreezing your computer screen to dealing with the VAT inspector.

Leaders all develop strong people skills. People skills include a myriad of capabilities covered in this book: delegating, motivating, influencing, resolving conflict, building teams, setting goals and leading change. For any aspiring leader, the challenge is to develop the people skills early: it is easier to experiment, mess up and change early in your career than when you find yourself suddenly leading an organization with over 1,000 people in it. Some organizations develop these people skills fast: the armed forces, teaching and many service sector jobs such as hotels, restaurants and clubs provide unique training grounds in dealing with the human animal.

EXERCISE 2.1 Are you on the right journey?

Are you learning great technical skills (dealing in bonds, accounting, law), which lead to a profession or to middle management?

Are you also learning how to get people to do things: delegating, coaching, resolving conflict, motivating, persuading, selling a vision and direction and leading?

This is the road to leadership.

Schools teach exactly the wrong sorts of skills
for becoming a leader.

02
Managing your leadership journey: the map

By now it should be clear that leadership means different things to different people in different organizations. It also means different things at different levels of an organization. This can become truly confusing, but there is a way through. Our research showed that, at each level of an organization, there are fundamentally different expectations of what a leader should look like and do. The differences are consistent across industries and countries, with some minor exceptions: in Japan they rate the ability to speak English as a key leadership requirement. If Anglo-Saxons could also learn to use English better, we would all be saved much drivel.

Take a look at Table 2.1. This table is based on original research asking followers what they expected of their leaders, and what percentage of them thought that leaders were delivering the desired quality. It shows the top five expectations of what a good leader looks like at each level of an organization (satisfaction ratings are shown in brackets). Note the following:

- Respondents all believed that you can lead at all levels of the organization: leadership is not the sole preserve of the CEO. To succeed, you need to develop and practise leadership skills from an early stage.

- Expectations of what good leaders look like change at each level. This explains why some people do very well at one level but then get altitude sickness at the next. To succeed, you need to adapt to new rules of success at each level.

Table 2.1 Top five expectations of leaders at all levels

Top leaders	Leaders in the middle	Recent graduates/ emerging leaders
Vision (61%)	Ability to motivate others (43%)	Hard work (64%)
Ability to motivate others (37%)	Decisiveness (54%)	Proactivity (57%)
Decisiveness (47%)	Industry experience (70%)	Intelligence (63%)
Ability to handle crises (56%)	Networking ability (57%)	Reliability (61%)
Honesty and integrity (48%)	Delegation (43%)	Ambition (64%)

- There is a large dissatisfaction with top leaders' ability to motivate others: only 37 per cent are satisfied with top leaders on this criterion.

- The performance expectations for emerging leaders are low and largely about behaviour: hard work, proactivity, reliability. Many aspiring leaders fall over these very low hurdles.

- The most divisive criterion was honesty and integrity. A boss who was rated well on this, and was therefore trusted, tended to be rated well on everything else. Bosses who rated poorly on this were damned on all other criteria.

The good news about these criteria is that you do not have to be superhuman to be a leader. The leadership requirements are simple and basic, and many people fail to live up to them. Focus on these basics, do them well and you will stand apart from many of your peer group.

> You do not have to be superhuman to be a leader.

03
Discover your rules of success

The rules of success and survival vary depending on your organization and its circumstances. Think of risk-taking: it is the lifeblood of an investment bank and it is like kryptonite to the Civil Service. In one context you cannot survive without risk-taking; in the other, risk-taking kills you.

Here is a critical, and deceptively difficult, exercise for you.

EXERCISE 2.2   Discovering the rules of success

What are the rules of success in your organization?

Hint one: Look at the people who get promoted and get the big bonuses. What do they do? Ignore the formal evaluation criteria, which are toys to keep the HR people happy.

Hint two: Think of the following sorts of trade-offs:

- Take risks versus make no mistakes.
- Achieve results versus follow the process.
- Do what the boss says versus exceed expectations.
- Be creative versus be reliable.
- Grow revenues versus control costs.
- Maximize profits versus maximize ethical pedigree.
- Be a selfless team player versus be a star.

- Put your liver on the line versus stay sober at all costs.
- Put in face time versus deliver the goods.
- Work in sales/finance/products/the company power base.
- Find the right sponsor/power baron/projects.
- Learn golf versus learn accounting.
- Many other criteria relevant to your context.

You may not like the rules of success in your organization. Selling your soul to succeed may not be worth it. If you do not like the rules of success, do not complain about them. Save your breath. You can adapt, leave or sulk.

Sulking is not a good route to leadership.

04
Build your career

Your career is a marathon, not a sprint, so plan it out well. Your greatest responsibility is for your own career.

Your most important task is to find the right role with the right employer and the right boss. If you have a lousy role with a lousy employer and a lousy boss, that is your problem and your responsibility. You can either whine about it or do something about it: many people choose to whine about it because that is easier. But if you are in the wrong job then you will go nowhere fast.

Over half of new graduates find that they are in the wrong job when they leave university, which gives rise to a productive first-bounce market for hiring good graduates with a couple of years' experience who want to start again. The bad news is that it is so easy to make the wrong call; the good news is that you are not alone and despite a tough economy, there is always demand for real talent.

So how can you spot the right employer, right role and right boss?

The right employer

Ask yourself some basic questions:

- Is the employer growing? It is easier to get promoted in an organization that is growing than in one that is contracting.
- Will growth continue? Some markets have been in long-term growth for 30 years (management consulting, for instance) and some firms have an inherent competitive advantage that assures growth.

How strong is the competition? Remember, the real competition is not another firm: it is sitting at a desk near you. If the firm recruits 1,000 graduates annually, ask how many of them go on to the top of the firm: probably only 1–10 per cent reach the top roles. Rest assured that the other 90 per cent also thought they would reach the top; work out the odds and place your bets accordingly.

- Will I build skills that will be useful for the future? Marketing, HR, accounting and sales are all very usable and transferable skills. Many employers seek these sorts of skills. If you become an expert in settlements in the tripartite asset-collateralized repo market, you have far fewer career choices ahead of you.

- Does this firm have a good reputation in the marketplace? If you join P&G in marketing you can find another job more easily than if you join Jim's Acme Widgets in marketing. How will this experience and employer look on my CV?

- Will I enjoy working here? You only excel at what you enjoy. And life is short. So make sure you work in a place you think you will enjoy.

- Will I succeed? Do I have the relevant aptitude to succeed? Do not try to fake it: if it works, you will regret it. Look hard at what successful people in the firm do to succeed and ask if that is the sort of person you are and you want to be.

The right role

Again, ask the right questions:

- Will I enjoy the work?

- Will I succeed? Do I have the right support, right budget and right expectations? If not, negotiate before you accept the role. Once you have accepted the role, all your negotiating power has disappeared.

- Will I develop skills that will help me for the future? Do not get caught in the comfort zone where you are asked to do the same sort of thing repeatedly. You will be very good at it but you become the 'boffin in the box': good at one line of expertise, but not building the management skills needed for promotion.

- Will this role give me a claim to fame? Does the role have any visibility two levels higher up the organization? Or will I be trapped in an obscure area doing worthy work and becoming completely overlooked?

The right boss

Every organization has bosses from hell and bosses from heaven. And everyone knows who they are. You can hope to get lucky in the assignment process, but hope is not a method and luck is not a strategy. You need to take control over your destiny and work the assignment process. That means finding out what opportunities are emerging and either becoming very visible or doing a Harry Potter: assume the cloak of invisibility and become completely unavailable. Most bosses are looking for loyal and effective team members: you do yourself no harm by flattering potential bosses and showing an interest in working for them. If necessary, put in some discretionary effort to help them out, and they are likely to repay your commitment when it comes to assignment time.

Finally, remember that there are three one-way leaps you can make in your career: once you have leapt, you cannot go back. These huge leaps are:

1 **Working for yourself.** Once you have tasted the freedom and frustration of being your own boss, you will find it very hard to go back into the confines of a system where you have lost control and you work for a boss you probably do not respect.

2 **Becoming a CEO (or partner in a professional services firm).** Like the self-employed, you will not be able to go back to working for others. Unlike the self-employed, you will have the option of disappearing off into committee and commission land in search of a gong.

3 **Moving off the gold standard.** There are a few gold-standard firms in any industry: GE, P&G or Unilever, McKinsey and Goldman Sachs. While you are there, countless other employers will want to snare you. Once you leave, you will struggle ever to get back to the gold standard those firms represent.

> Your career is a marathon, not a sprint.

05
Careers versus careering: avoiding the death stars

For some people, 'career' is a noun that describes a steady progression from fresh-faced graduate to a happy retirement. For others, 'career' is a verb that describes a chaotic slalom through myriad adventures on the path to leadership or disaster. Whether you want a career or prefer to career, it pays to avoid death star organizations, projects and bosses. Traditionally, these are known as CLM for good reasons: they are Career Limiting Moves.

Death star organizations

You take a huge gamble when you join an organization. You can improve the odds if you join an organization that is likely to grow and succeed. Put simply, there are more opportunities for promotion in an organization growing at 20 per cent a year than in one declining by 20 per cent a year.

Do your research. Today's winners may not be tomorrow's winners. Anyone joining a telecoms company around 1985 would have joined a fixed-line company, not any of the small start-ups selling mobiles – which looked like bricks and weighed like bricks – to loud-mouthed and loudly dressed property developers. There have been many more opportunities with the mobile companies than with fixed-line operators over the last 30 years.

Death star projects

Ask yourself two questions before taking on an assignment: 1) is the assignment worthwhile? and 2) is the assignment set up for success?

A worthwhile assignment is one that has relevance and impact at least two levels up the organization (unless you are already the CEO). Ideally, it will also be close to the centre of power. Being asked to run the business in Japan is exciting, but after three years everyone back in your home country will have forgotten that you exist. Your new bosses will not know what promises were made when you left: fulfilling other people's promises to you will be very low on their list of priorities. Stay close to the centre of power.

An assignment is set up for success if it has the four following characteristics:

1 **The right sponsor.** If the project is relevant to someone two levels up, that person will be actively promoting and supporting it. This makes it worthwhile, and politically it makes it more likely to succeed.

2 **The right problem.** Politically, any CEO problem is the right problem because you know it will get the visibility and support to make it succeed. In practice, you need to use judgement. Spending a year fixing the wrong problem is not a good career investment.

3 **The right team and resources.** If the assignment is under-resourced or understaffed, then it is clearly not a real priority; worse, it is not likely to succeed.

4 **The right process.** Working against insane deadlines, needing double and triple checks before sneezing and testing either everything or nothing are not good success recipes.

Finally, consider whether you are the right person for the job. Doing competitive research on the Thai tapioca industry appeals to some people and some people are very good at that sort of thing. Do not be lured by the prospect of doing tapioca research on a tropical island: consider very carefully whether you will actually be able to deliver a great result.

Avoiding death star projects is not always easy. Here are some basic principles:

- **Switch your radar on.** Keep on the lookout for what are the emerging assignments and opportunities. Talk to everyone: gossip is good.

- **Assume the cloak of invisibility when a death star assignment looms.** Make sure that you are very busy elsewhere. Start making yourself useful by volunteering to do things for bosses: do someone a favour. That person will appreciate it, and you will be curiously unavailable when the death star assignment is being staffed.

- **Avoid succeeding too much at things you do not like.** If you are really good at developing business cases to justify systems changes in the life insurance industry, you may find that your pigeonhole becomes a career coffin: you will not be allowed to do anything else.

- **Make yourself very useful to people who have interesting assignments.** Volunteer to do stuff for them. Express an active interest in the assignments that tick your boxes: they will then work the formal system to get you assigned.

- **Last and least, work the formal assignment system.** HR people will tell you how the assignment system works. Their rational world of assignment systems tends to be overwhelmed by the political reality of bosses fighting to get the best staff on to their books. Work the politics hard, but try to avoid upsetting the HR people too much in the process.

Death star bosses

Death star bosses come in four unpalatable flavours: too strong, too weak, the wrong taste or the wrong menu:

1 Too strong bosses. These are the Darth Vader types who demand your soul. There is some good news about them: they will look after their team very protectively. But the moment you flinch or you fail to deliver, you are dead meat. You are 100 per cent in or 100 per cent out. They tend to chew up and spit out team members at an alarming rate.

2 **Too weak bosses.** These may feel easy to work with, but at crunch time they are often unable to deliver on expectations on pay, promotions and assignments.

3 **The wrong taste.** The wrong taste may simply be a matter of two styles that are too alike (two introverts with nothing to say to each other or two egos that take up too much space in the room). Or it may be a problem of two conflicting styles that cannot work together. Do the Style Compass to figure out what it will take to succeed with a boss.

4 **Wrong menu.** Even if everything else is right about the boss, if he or she is working in the wrong part of the organization you will be in trouble. From your perspective, the wrong part of the organization is one where either you are unlikely to succeed or there is limited career progression.

Avoid succeeding too much at things you do not like.

06
How not to get promoted

If you are in the right role with the right boss you are at least in the race for promotion. If you have the wrong role and wrong boss you are not even in the race.

In an ideal world, if you worked hard, beat your targets and had a good attitude you would get promoted. We do not live in an ideal world. A quick look at colleagues who do and do not get promoted will tell you that working hard and beating targets are not enough to get you promoted. You need to do more.

Ask for promotion. If you don't ask the question, you don't get the answer. And even if the answer is 'No' that leads into a productive conversation about what you need to do to get promoted. Some people are happy to push themselves, others are not: the pushy types trample the less pushy. Ugly, but true.

Build your claim to fame. You can be sure that lots of your colleagues have worked hard and beaten targets. You need to do something that is seen and valued at least two levels above you. You need visibility beyond your boss, otherwise you depend solely on his or her word and reputation.

Be visible, be positive. There are always projects, issues, speeches or reports where people higher up the food chain need help: be the one who goes the extra mile to help them. Volunteer and make yourself useful to senior people.

Make the most of any opportunities you have in front of top people: they will judge you not on the one year of hard work you have done in the background, but on the three minutes when you were presenting to them, talking to them or meeting them. Make the most of your moments of truth.

Don't wait until you are ready for promotion. It will be an eternal wait. No one is ever ready for the challenges one level above them. Be bold. Seek promotion early and believe in your own ability to grow into the job. If you wait, be ready to get trampled in the rush of less-qualified people racing straight past you on their way to the top.

There are plenty of ways to make sure you do not get promoted. Here are a few of the classics:

- **Disloyalty.** Don't get too political about trying to replace your boss. Bosses forgive most sins, but disloyalty is not one of them.

- **Incompetence.** If you have a gold medal in incompetence, nothing will save you.

- **Values and attitude.** Most people get hired for their technical skills, but fired for their lack of values or people skills. Every organization has informal rules of the game, which are never written down. Work out what the real values and real rules are and play to those. If you do not like the values or the informal rules, you may well be in the wrong organization.

Build your claim to fame.

07
Knowing when to move on

Every career has its peaks and troughs. The troughs are not just tough; they are also very often lonely. In success you have friends; in setbacks, you are often all alone. These are critical moments. The difference between failure and success is often as simple as giving up. The people who reach the top are not always the best and the brightest: they just kept going. In sailing, they say that 'to finish first, first you must finish'. There is no point in going fast if you capsize.

But equally, if you are in a dead end and are getting nowhere however hard you push, when should you move on?

First, there is a poor but very common reason for moving on: you fall out with your boss. Most people do not leave their firms, they leave their boss. In large firms, this can be a mistake. The corporate carousel keeps on turning, which means that no boss is for ever: there are restructurings, you or they get moved or promoted. If your problem is your boss, you may want to look at alternatives within the same firm, before jumping ship.

There are real dangers to jumping ship. Headhunters will always paint a picture where the grass is greener elsewhere. Remember that it is greenest where it rains the most. A prospective employer will always put on their best face to you. But all firms suffer the same problems: politics, crises, dull work, career hazards. The wonderful boss who hires you could soon be replaced by Attila the Hun's alter ego.

When you are in a tough place, listen to your head and heart. But make sure you ask them the right questions. Here are three questions for you to ask.

1 What do I enjoy?

Ask your heart the most important question: what do I really enjoy doing? Don't ask 'do I enjoy my current position?' because the answer will just depress you. Ask your heart the bigger question of what you do enjoy. Most people, despite claims to the contrary, enjoy work: it gives them a sense of purpose and a sense of community. It also pays the bills. So what sort of work do you enjoy?

Asking what you enjoy may seem frivolous, but it is not. You only excel at what you enjoy. To excel at anything you have to put in huge effort, discretionary effort. We can all put in extra effort for a month or two in a crisis, even with things we do not enjoy that much. But to excel over a career requires discretionary effort over years and decades. You can only sustain that effort if you gain satisfaction from what you do. So work out what you enjoy, and then work out what sort of work and context will meet your needs. That may or may not be in your current firm.

2 Am I set up for success?

This is really a two-part question. First, do your homework on your current or prospective employer. Are they set up for success? Are they going to be growing or declining over the next 10 years? Bluntly, growth means opportunity and decline means stress. Back a winner.

Then ask if you are in a role which has potential, and whether that role is set up with the right support, management and resources to enable you to succeed. If not, then work to get it set up right. All battles are won or lost before the first shot is fired. There is no point in fighting valiantly if you are not set up to succeed.

3 What will I learn?

A career is a marathon, not a sprint. In the long term, success is determined by the skills you acquire. The skills you need tomorrow are different from the skills you need today. So you can sprint ahead today by using the skills you already have, but you will soon find that you are running nowhere. Meanwhile, the people who invest in the careers and their learning slowly move ahead. Learning does not mean formal training and courses, although these help. Learning is as much about having the right experiences and being exposed to the best sorts of managers and leaders whom you can watch and learn from. Ask yourself where you are most likely to get the right bosses and right experience.

As you ask yourself these questions you will inevitably find that you get contradictory answers. That's life. At times like this, it pays to get help. You need to talk to someone: it could be a coach, a family member or friend. Often, the simple act of talking about these questions makes the answers obvious. Then find the courage to make it happen.

Remember, it is greenest where it rains the most.

08
Coach yourself to success

How do you learn about what works and what does not? Pick two of the six possible sources of learning:

- books;
- courses;
- bosses (good and bad);
- peers;
- role models (inside and outside work);
- experience.

Most people choose direct experience. Virtually no one chooses books or courses, which is bad news for authors.

There are two problems about learning from experience. First, experience takes time and most of us want to progress fast. Second, experience is a random walk. If you are lucky and get good bosses and role models, you accelerate your career. Bad experiences and bosses drive you straight into a dead end.

So how can you accelerate and structure your learning? The traditional answer is to hire a coach. But they are expensive and of variable quality. What you need is the best coach in the world: someone who understands you and your situation. You need to hire yourself.

Coach yourself by following the plan–do–review cycle on all your activities:

- **Plan** what you want to achieve and how. The simple act of stopping and thinking for 30 seconds before picking up the phone can make all the difference. Most people understand the need to plan and think ahead, except when they are caught in the heat of battle and emotions are running high: that is when cool thinking is most needed.

- **Do it.** This should be obvious but it is not. Sending e-mails, looking at the internet and attending meetings are often a good alternative to work if you have time on your hands. Planning should eliminate these wastes and help you focus on real work.

- **Review it.** Most executives are useless at this. They may start a post mortem when things go wrong, but often that is playing the blame game, not the learning game. But the review stage is where you learn most and it is your chance to accelerate your career. It is your secret weapon.

Here is how to review effectively, and it need only take a few seconds of your time. After any key event, ask yourself two questions:

1 **WWW**: What went well? Again, most people forget to think about what went well. We assume that success is the natural state of affairs. Success is not natural. Making things happen is very hard work, and there are endless obstacles which stand in our way. So when things work well, step back and ask 'why? what did I do that helped things work well?' This is how you will build your personal success formula.

2 **EBI**: Even better if. When things go awry it is easy, but pointless, to beat ourselves up about it. So don't look for the evil twin of WWW: what went wrong. That will simply depress you. Instead, ask what you could have done differently, or tried to make things work better. Then, next time you are in a similar situation, you will have a new strategy to try out. You may even succeed.

You can do WWW and EBI with team members after meetings. You can also do it privately and informally in your head as you walk down the corridor. At first, it will seem cumbersome. Over time, it will become like second nature.

You do not need to accumulate experience; you need to accumulate learning. WWW and EBI are your key to learning and success.

09
Running the leadership marathon

One eminent business school professor claims that leadership is not a sprint; it is a marathon run in a series of 400-metre sprints. This shows that he is clueless about how to run a marathon. But, fortunately, he has more insight into leadership than he does marathons. With a few notable exceptions, who are normally successful entrepreneurs, it takes decades to reach a senior leadership position. Leaders, like actors, take many years to become an overnight success.

The question for all aspiring leaders is how to build and sustain the stamina required for the leadership marathon. The strategic answer was hinted at in an earlier section: you only excel at what you enjoy. Life is too short to do things you hate, even if they pay well. You will eventually stress out, burn out and drop out to start your organic pig farm in Wales. That is not the road to leadership. Whatever you do, enjoy it. Even if you do not succeed on the leadership journey, at least you will have enjoyed the trip.

The deeper answer is to look after yourself. This is where we enter the murky waters of wellbeing gurus, lifestyle gurus and ultimately power crystals, healing and feng shui.

EXERCISE 2.3   The stress test

- Do you regularly work more than 50 hours a week?
- Do you take less than four weeks' holiday a year?
- Do you let work come into your holidays and social/home life?

- Do you drink more than 12 units of alcohol a week (1 pint = 2 units)?
- Do you smoke or take any other drugs?
- Do you feel tired often and/or have trouble getting to sleep?
- Do you get lots of small illnesses?
- Do you have more responsibility than authority, or a lack of control?

Try to balance your life so that not too many answers are 'Yes'.

Work–life balance is not code for letting people go off and start families. It is about allowing you to create and sustain the energy that will carry you to the top, not to the pig farm. Here are some obvious suggestions:

- **Diet.** The right foods make a big difference. You do not need to be a crank, but a diet of greasy burgers and chips is a heart attack on a plate: it is not worth it.
- **Exercise.** Find something you enjoy. Imitating a hamster on a treadmill is not for everyone.
- **Enjoyment.** All the leaders we researched clearly enjoyed what they did. If there is stress, it is in the middle of the organization, not at the top.
- **Relaxation.** Most leaders are not one-dimensional. They tend to have active interests outside work, which may be physical (hiking, skiing, sailing), intellectual and cultural (arts, clubs) or social.
- **Sleep.** Turn up to work drunk and you can expect to be fired. Turn up tired, and it is a badge of honour. But the effects of tiredness on decision making, reactions and self-awareness are just the same as the effects of drinking.
- **Switch-off time.** Switch off the computer, text messages, phone, e-mail and all the other technology that imprisons you into a 24/7 work style. You do not have to work at 2 am while you are meant to be on holiday.

Find what works for you. Remember that, just as the mind controls the body, so the body controls the mind. Try clenching your fists and jaw and then relaxing them: the difference is immediate. Breathing exercises and mild meditation can work wonders.

Work–life balance is desirable but dangerous if it is simply an excuse to work less. The answer is not to avoid work: the answer is to find work that you enjoy, that leads you where you want to go and that has meaning and relevance to you. Leadership is hard work: you cannot shortcut to leadership by working less.

You only excel at what you enjoy.

10
Staying employable

Career is both a noun and a verb. For most people, career used to be a noun. It described how you joined a firm as a young person and then left 45 years later with a carriage clock and a defined benefit pension. You would then show your gratitude to your faithful employer by promptly dying so that you did not overload their generous pension scheme.

Career is now a verb for most people. It describes how we have to slalom from one opportunity to the next. Each employer will require us to show 100 per cent passion, 110 per cent commitment, 120 per cent loyalty and 130 per cent integrity. They will be 100 per cent loyal to us, until the day they need to restructure, downsize, outsource, right size, offshore, best shore or plain fire us. And that can happen at any time.

The result of the shift of career from noun to verb is that employment no longer comes from our employer; it comes from our employability. We have to have the right skills and experience if we want to stay in meaningful work.

Keeping the right skills is a challenge. As a test, ask yourself what the following have in common:

- camel jockeys;
- Japanese waitresses;
- Korean baseball fans;
- New York stockbrokers.

Answer: they have all been replaced by robots or computers. Oxford University estimates that over half of all current jobs can be replaced by robots. Being a white collar worker does not protect you. You may do work that requires intelligence, but computers are learning fast. When managers talk about 'business sense' they often mean pattern recognition. Smart managers have seen that movie before and they know what they need to do next. Computer intelligence is also about pattern recognition, and they are getting very good at it.

Even if you are not replaced by a robot, the skills you need today are not the skills you need tomorrow. Clearly, this is a threat. It is also a huge opportunity. In the old world of employment, you had security but no freedom. You did what your employer told you to do, and you progressed slowly. In the new world, we have lost security but gained freedom. We can do what we want, provided we work for it.

There are three keys to staying employable in the new world of insecure freedom.

1 **Keep on learning.** Never stop learning and adapting. Never. Keep looking ahead to see what skills you will need for your next role or your next promotion. Those are the skills you need. At some point in your career, you may well need to reinvent yourself. If that happens, be brave. Take the chance to learn a new set of skills and enjoy the chance to start careering.

2 **Build your track record.** It is not enough to have worked hard. Many people work hard and are then laid off. You need a claim to fame. You need to show that you have achieved something over and above what might have been expected for someone in your role. This claim to fame has the obvious benefit of making you more attractive to employers, including your current employer. It has the less obvious benefit that any claim to fame involves pushing yourself into new territory. That means you were probably learning and growing fast.

3 **Build your networks.** If you have a good network within your current firm, you will know in advance where the good opportunities are, and where the death star assignments and bosses are likely to emerge. You can then take evasive action as necessary. And if you are well networked and well supported, then you are

likely to be towards the bottom of the list when it comes to lay offs and restructurings. Your external networks are also vital. Most jobs are filled through personal networks. Even where there is a formal search, the search is often doing little more than confirming an informal decision made by your network.

Never stop learning and adapting. Never.

Part Three
People skills

01
Understand yourself

As a leader, understanding yourself does not require seeing a guru in India, gazing at your navel or discussing your childhood with a shrink. It requires that you understand how you affect other people. Do not worry about what box shrinks try to put you in. Boxes are for the dead, not the living. You only need to worry about how you affect others. If you understand this, then you understand what matters about yourself.

You need some way of understanding yourself and how you affect others and, for better or worse, there are many psychological models and tools to help you or, in some cases, confuse and depress you. The Myers–Briggs Type Indicator (MBTI) is very much the tool *du jour*. It takes many years to become an expert at it, which defeats its own purpose. The idea is not to become an MBTI expert: it is to become a leader.

The received wisdom about all these models, including MBTI, is that there is no 'bad' category. This is a fiction used by facilitators who want an easy time with the groups they lead. Like the astrologers who always give positive horoscopes, they do not want to upset paying customers. All the categories in MBTI have a positive and a negative side. You affect people both positively and negatively with your style, and it pays to understand both sides. Table 3.1 shows a revisionist version of MBTI.

Critics of MBTI complain that it lacks any serious peer-reviewed academic credibility. They are narrowly right but broadly wrong. MBTI is not there to help people become psychiatrists. It is a simple tool to make you aware of and respect different ways of working. Many of these differences make a team stronger by preventing group think.

Table 3.1   Myers–Briggs Type Indicator (MBTI) outline

Type	Description	Positive impact	Negative impact
Extroversion (E)	Gains energy from others. Speaks then thinks.	Spreads energy, enthusiasm.	Loudmouth. Does not include other people.
Introversion (I)	Gains energy from within. Thinks before speaking.	Thoughtful. Gives space to others.	Nothing worth saying? Uneasy networker.
Sensing (S)	Observes outside world. More facts, fewer ideas.	Practical, concrete, detailed.	Dull, unimaginative.
Intuitive (N)	Pays attention to self, inner world, ideas.	Creative, imaginative.	Flighty, impractical, unrealistic.
Thinking (T)	Decides with head and logic.	Logical, rational, intellectual.	Cold and heartless.
Feeling (F)	Listens to the heart.	Empathetic, understanding.	Soft-headed, fuzzy thinker, bleeding heart.
Judging (J)	Organized, scheduled, tidy.	High work ethic. Focused and reliable.	Compulsive neat freak. Uptight, rigid, rule-bound.
Perceiving (P)	Keeps options open. Opportunistic.	Work–life balance. Enjoys work.	Lazy, messy, aimless and unreliable.

EXERCISE 3.1   Discovering your style

Your first exercise is to figure out where you are on MBTI.

As you look at the list of positive characteristics, you will naturally believe you have all of them. You will discover the truth you long suspected: you are perfect. MBTI does not let you off so lightly. You have to choose between E and I, between S and N, between T and F and between J and P. The result is that in the world of MBTI you become an ugly acronym like ENTP, or ISFJ, or INFP.

If you are still having difficulty discovering your style, look at the negative impact column in the MBTI chart. You will probably discover quickly what you are least like.

Now do the same for your boss. Putting the boss in the right negative boxes is pretty easy for most people.

Boxes are for the dead, not the living.

02
Understand others

The pay-off from using MBTI comes when you use it to influence others effectively. A good team will be a mix of styles. If everyone is an introvert, the room will echo to the sound of silence. If everyone is an extrovert, the room will be rowdier than a chimpanzees' tea party. These odd combinations are productive, but hard to maintain. A common trade-off is between the Thinking types and the Feeling types.

Thinkers often focus only on tasks and actions; feelers will speak of little other than people. You need a team that can manage both the tasks and the people, and you need to recognize that the different styles of each team member are valuable. Table 3.2 shows how to deal with the different types of person.

Table 3.2 Dealing with different MBTI types

Your type	Their type	How they may see you	How you can adjust
Extroversion (E)	Introvert	Loudmouth. Does not include other people.	Give others time to think and to speak. Ask open questions.
Introversion (I)	Extrovert	Nothing worth saying? Uneasy networker.	Prepare in advance to have something to say.
Sensing (S)	Intuitive	Dull, unimaginative.	Take over some of the practical detail that intuitive types dislike.

(continued)

Table 3.2 *(Continued)*

Your type	Their type	How they may see you	How you can adjust
Intuitive (N)	Sensing	Flighty, impractical, unrealistic.	Ask for help on practical things: form an alliance with a sensing person.
Thinking (T)	Feeling	Cold and heartless.	Try to win a friend, not just win an argument.
Feeling (F)	Thinking	Soft-headed, fuzzy thinker, bleeding heart.	Let the thinkers think; then work the people and the politics.
Judging (J)	Perceiving	Compulsive neat freak. Uptight, rigid, rule-bound.	Ignore the chaos; quietly focus on the substantive battles.
Perceiving (P)	Judging	Lazy, messy, aimless and unreliable.	Clear up the mess on the desk and make sure the report gets in on time.

There are a few principles hidden in here:

- **Do not try to be someone else.** If you are an introvert, then you are not suddenly going to transform yourself into an extrovert who is the life and soul of the party. Under stress, people often resort to a second style of operation. This is often catastrophic: they have had less practice at that style, and the outcome is rarely good. Be true to yourself.

- **Do not try to change the other person.** Understand how the other person's style differs from yours. These differences are positive.

Together, you are likely to be able to achieve more than if you operate independently. An intuitive person will have many ideas and a sensing person will be very practical on the detail. One of you is the guru with the vision; the other is the commissar who can work out how to make the vision real. It is a powerful leadership combination.

- **Be patient.** If you are highly task-focused (T) it can be frustrating if someone else never talks about the critical tasks in hand. Instead this person talks about people the whole time. The person is an F. This is a good combination: one of you works out what needs to be done (T); the other works on the politics and people (F) to enable it to happen.

- **Be aware.** Most of us stumble into personal and professional relationships. We know how long it takes to build personal relationships. We have little time to build professional relationships. We need to understand other people's styles fast so that we can influence them positively and quickly.

- **Find the right situation in which to work.** Warren Buffet remarked that 'when a great manager joins a lousy company, it is normally the reputation of the company that remains intact'. The same is true of work styles: you will not change the style of the organization in which you work. You need to find a way of living with the style of your organization, or you need a new organization.

> When a great manager joins a lousy company, it is normally the reputation of the company that remains intact.

- **Build the team.** Strong teams are diverse. Diversity means more than diversity of race, gender, age and faith. It means the subtler diversity of building a team with complementary styles, skills and perspectives. A football team of 11 great goalkeepers is unlikely to do well.

> A football team of 11 great goalkeepers is unlikely to do well.

03
Understand how you affect others

L eadership requires getting other people to do things. It often means getting others to do things they would rather not do: for some people, working for you may not be as attractive as having a family life and meeting friends.

Some leaders think you lead by coercion. Coercion can be remarkably effective in the short term. When a mugger held a knife to my neck and asked for my money, I duly obliged. The mugger made me do something I preferred not to do, but he was not an ideal leadership role model. He had achieved compliance, not commitment.

Coercion and compliance were standard leadership models in the 19th century when bosses bossed and workers worked. In the 21st century there is a better educated and more demanding workforce, which requires a different form of leadership. We all have suffered at the hands of bosses who are still stuck in the 19th century. Bossing people is lazy leadership; increasingly it is ineffective leadership.

To be an effective leader, you need to move beyond coercion and compliance. You need to be able to gain the commitment and support of the people you lead. You cannot gain their commitment if you do not understand them and you do not understand how you affect them.

We have seen from MBTI that understanding people can be a full-time profession. In practice, we do not have time to do a full psychological audit of each person we meet. As practising leaders, we need some shortcuts to help us make sense of who we are meeting and how they are behaving.

The Style Compass™ is a quick and easy way of thinking about how to influence someone. In this exercise, think of someone you are trying to influence. You should get plenty of practice with your boss, so try them.

EXERCISE 3.2   The Style Compass

Step 1 is to decide what the important aspects are of the person's character. Here are some typical characteristics that practising leaders have identified as being important in the people they deal with:

- people focused versus task focused;
- process focused versus outcome focused;
- risk tolerant versus risk averse;
- big picture versus detail;
- words versus numbers;
- oral versus written communication;
- inductive versus deductive;
- tactful versus blunt;
- sensitive versus thick skinned;
- controlling versus empowering;
- quick versus slow;
- open versus defensive;
- morning versus afternoon;
- positive versus cynical;
- analysis versus action.

Here are a few more dimensions that different shrinks believe are important. These dimensions have considerable analytical rigour behind them, and each branch of psychology promotes its own set of dimensions as being the only true, meaningful and relevant dimensions. You decide which ones you find most useful:

- intellectual versus instinctual;
- withdrawn versus attached;
- idealistic versus practical;
- alert versus settled;
- progressive versus conservative;
- non-traditional versus traditional;
- future oriented versus past oriented;
- congenial versus coercive;
- solicitous versus antagonistic;
- receptive versus assertive;
- submissive versus domineering;
- acceptance seeking versus pleasure seeking;
- sensitive versus insensitive;
- socialistic versus materialistic.

Step 2 is to plot the person's characteristics on the Compass, as illustrated in Figure 3.1.

Figure 3.1 The Style Compass for my boss

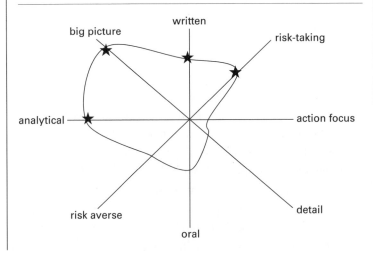

As you plot the Style Compass, focus on what is most important about the other person, not about yourself. The dimensions can be anything you think is most important. In this case, the stars show I think my boss is very analytical, likes the big picture, is a risk-taker and prefers written communications.

Step 3 is to plot yourself on your boss's Style Compass (see Figure 3.2, where your boss is the solid line and you the dotted line). If you are well aligned you are lucky; more likely, you will have to figure out how to get on the boss's wavelength.

Figure 3.2   The Style Compass: my boss compared to me

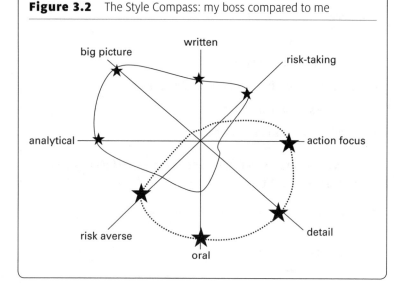

In the example above, my boss and I are very different. This could make us a very effective but difficult working combination. After drawing this Style Compass, I realize that I need to adapt to get on the wavelength of my boss. I need to produce more written material: the boss feels more comfortable with that than with oral briefings. I just need to focus on the big picture, and be sure to give plenty of analytical reasons why the big picture is the right one. I also need to curb my instinct to plunge into doing lots of practical things until the big picture has been agreed, otherwise the boss will think I may be wasting my time doing the wrong thing. Naturally, I think the boss is wasting time analysing all the big stuff when we could be moving to action. When I am the boss, things will change. But in the meantime, I get to play by the boss's rules, not mine.

> The mugger was not an ideal leadership role model. He had achieved compliance, not commitment.

04
Delegating

People do not like delegating. It often means:

- loss of personal control;
- time 'wasted' explaining, coaching and correcting;
- unexpected outcomes, and dilution of personal standards;
- stress from loss of control.

Effective delegation frees your time to focus on where you add most value and helps develop the skills of your team. Failure to delegate traps you into doing low-level jobs. You cannot lead if you cannot delegate. Here is why you must delegate:

- Delegation is the only way to create more than 24 hours in a day. If you don't delegate, you work yourself into an early grave.

- Delegation allows you to focus on the areas where you make the most difference. It forces you to stretch yourself: you have to learn new skills rather than simply doing your last job better.

- It shows you have trust in the team, and most teams will respond to your vote of confidence in them by working hard to show they are worthy of your trust.

- It builds and stretches your team: they have to learn new skills.

How not to delegate

The easy way to work out how to delegate well is to reflect on the worst experiences you have suffered from poor delegation – then do the opposite. Here is the delegation style of one boss from the Museum of Management Malpractice. For legal reasons we will let 'Jim' stay anonymous.

Jim would only delegate three sorts of activities:

1 **Routine rubbish**. Delegating the administrivia freed him to do the important things, like working out how to get promoted.

2 **Hospital passes**. Whenever he had a project going horribly wrong, he would delegate it to a subordinate as a 'development opportunity'. When the project duly collapsed, he would walk away and leave the subordinate crushed under the collapse. You can delegate most things. But you can never delegate away your responsibility, and you should never delegate the blame. Delegating blame makes you look weak and creates an atmosphere of fear and politicking.

3 **Last-minute panics**. Fridays were good days to avoid Jim. He would be thinking of the weekend and of all the work he had not done: time to delegate it all, especially if the deadline was Monday morning. Goodbye, weekend; hello, office.

Jim also had a unique style of delegation. He seemed to have three main principles:

1 Be vague about the objectives, and then change his mind several times in the course of the project. This would double the effort and halve the morale of the team.

2 Be vague about deadlines, but bring them forward by several days at the last moment just to keep everyone on their toes.

3 Be vague about the process in terms of how to do it, the support available, the critical path and the checkpoints. This gave him carte blanche to interfere at will with sudden and extreme demands at any point in the process.

On no account would he ever discuss any of this with the team. He saw himself as a strong manager, which meant that he liked to issue commands, preferably with elaborate detail on what the consequences of failure would look like.

Principles of effective delegation are:

- Ensure clarity of the task and the eventual success criteria.

- Make the team summarize back to you what they think the task and outcomes are meant to be. Do not assume they have understood anything until they say it back to you.

- Ensure people have enough skills and resources to complete the job: do not delegate too much too soon.

- Be clear about how you want to work together (progress reports). Discuss concerns before you start.

- Be available to help, but do not interfere all the time. When they ask for help, require them to suggest solutions so that they always learn.

- Delegate meaningful projects, not just administrivia. Stretch people and they will rise to the challenge. Giving away mundane jobs only demotivates people.

- Show faith and trust in the team: praise successes and do not undermine them.

- Remember, you may have delegated authority, but you cannot delegate away responsibility. You are still accountable for the outcomes.

EXERCISE 3.3 Effective delegation

Review the tasks you undertake, and allocate each one to one of the four sections of the delegation chart in Table 3.3. Then act on the outcomes.

Table 3.3 Delegation chart

	Others could do this	Only I can do this
Very Important	Delegate – supervise and support closely.	Take the lead – involve others so they can learn and develop.
Less Important	Delegate – make sure you are delegating more than just the rubbish.	Are you sure? Could be a development opportunity for someone.

As you fill in the chart, do not ask 'Are they capable of doing it today?' but ask 'Could they do it with enough help, support and supervision?' Your goal is not just to do the job, but also to stretch and develop your staff. You will be surprised by how much your team can achieve with the right support: people tend to rise or fall to the level of expectations set for them. So set high expectations and have the courage to delegate extensively. This has the added advantages of making your life easier and making you more popular with your team: they will see that you trust them and are developing them.

People do not like delegating.

05
Motivating

Theory X and Theory Y

Many trees have been destroyed by the motivation industry. The less fortunate among us also have had to endure motivational workshops. This is where a man (it is usually a man) in a white suit whips the audience up into a frenzy of excitement that lasts for as long as it takes for the attendees to reach the car park on the way home. Motivation is where shrinks go mad with their academic theories. Have they not yet heard of chocolate?

To save you from the dangerous men in white coats or white suits, we will explore three theories of motivation and then look at how the theories work in practice.

EXERCISE 3.4   Applying theory to your reality

Think of one of your bosses and decide whether he or she is an X type or Y type of person (see Table 3.4). Do the same for a few of your colleagues.

X and Y represent two ways of thinking about human motivation, as described in the classic *Human Side of Enterprise* by Douglas McGregor (1960, McGraw-Hill, New York). Now match the X- and Y-type categories to two different contexts: 1) a 19th-century

Table 3.4 X types and Y types

Management criteria	X-type manager	Y-type leader
Basis of power	Formal authority	Authority and respect
Focus of control	Process compliance	Outcomes, achievement
Communication style	One-way: tell and do	Two-way: tell and listen
Success criteria	Make no mistakes	Beat targets
Attention to detail	High	Moderate
Ambiguity tolerance	Minimal	Moderate
Political ability	Moderate	High
Preferred structure	Hierarchy	Network

sweatshop, with the workers paid piece rates and hired for their hands, not their heads, and clear, simple jobs with clear outcomes and targets; 2) a 21st-century service firm with high skills, ambiguity about how things should be done and a need for workers to use their heads more than their hands.

It should be fairly clear that theory Y fits many, but not all, current work contexts. But, in practice, many bosses find it easier to use theory X: it looks tough, sounds good and is easy to deploy. Think for a moment:

- How do you prefer to be led?
- How in practice do you lead other people?
- What would you change?
- How do your staff prefer to be led?

Avoid dangerous men in white coats or white suits.

Maslow

We all have hopes and fears, and good leaders know how to tap into them. This stunning piece of common sense was wrapped up into a nice psychological theory by Maslow, now known as 'Maslow's hierarchy of needs'. His basic argument is that we are all needs junkies. As soon as we have satisfied our basic needs for food and shelter we start realizing we have other needs. This makes sense in the ordinary world. One hundred years ago no one really thought that telephones, televisions, computers, cars, refrigerators, games consoles, iPads and pepperoni pizzas were necessities. A short conversation with a modern teenager will quickly establish that life is impossible without these essentials.

In business, people are also needs junkies. People in a company near to bankruptcy want a leader who can remove fear and create job security. The leader of a big company is probably thinking of his knighthood and leaving a legacy before he is forgotten completely. People have different needs in different contexts.

Figure 3.3   Maslow's hierarchy of needs (the unauthorized, revisionist, leadership version)

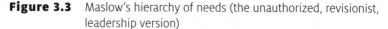

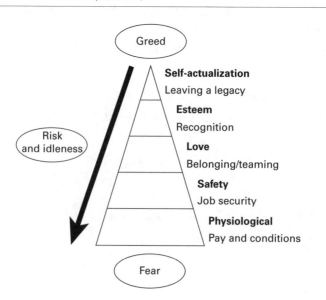

To make the theory digestible, there are three versions of it in Figure 3.3. The original version is in bold typeface, the leadership version is below the bold in normal typeface and the simplified, revisionist version is in the oval shapes. People climb the ladder from the bottom: they do not aspire to leave a legacy if they are still in fear of losing their jobs. Equally, as soon as they have achieved one level, they want to achieve the next, as long as the leader can make it easy for them: we may all want to be famous footballers, but it does take quite a lot of work.

> We are all needs junkies.

EXERCISE 3.5   Motivating: Putting Maslow to work

Where are you on Maslow's hierarchy? Where do you want to get to? Will your current context allow you to get there? What are you going to do about it?

In the next meeting you go to, see if you can spot where your colleagues are on the hierarchy. This may be difficult, so try something simpler. As you persuade them to do something, work out if you are appealing to:

- Their greed (hopes, ambitions, ability to complete a job).
- Their fears. (If they don't agree, the sky will fall down and they will not get promoted. If something is risky, they will resist. Show that the risk of doing nothing is greater than the risk of agreeing.)
- Their idleness. Make it easy for them to agree, and awkward for them to disagree.
- What the risks are of doing something. If you can remove risk, you will make it much easier for them to agree to what you want.

As an exercise, always try to figure out how to appeal to fear, greed and idleness. Work out how to reduce the perceived risk of your idea. If people are resisting you, work out which of fear, greed, idleness and risk is out of balance.

Think of your top team member. Where is he or she on Maslow's hierarchy? What are the hopes you can play on? How can you raise expectations even further?

Think of your lowest-performing team member. Where is he or she on Maslow's hierarchy? What are this person's fears and concerns? What can you do to ease those fears and concerns?

Appeal to fear, greed and idleness.

Management practice

Theory is good. Reality is better, or at least more useful, for leaders. Our research found five drivers of motivation in the workplace. The good news is that none of the drivers is magical or difficult to understand (though they may be difficult to put into practice). They are common sense, which is why they are so rare; they are:

1 My boss shows an interest in my career.

2 I trust my boss; he/she is honest with me.

3 I know where we are going and how to get there.

4 I am doing a worthwhile job.

5 I am recognized for my contribution.

If your team agrees with these statements, the chances are that they will also think you are smart and caring, have insight and are dynamic. They may even think you are witty and good looking.

If they disagree with the statements, they will damn you on all the other leadership criteria as well. Naturally, being seen to be a good boss with your team is not the same as impressing your bosses and delivering outstanding performance. But it is much easier to perform well with a team that supports and respects you than it is with a team that is alienated and demoralized.

EXERCISE 3.6 Assess yourself (and anyone else you want to)

Use these five drivers of motivation to assess yourself on how well you motivate. It may help to look in more detail at each driver:

1 **My boss shows an interest in my career**.
   - Do you know what ambitions your staff have?
   - When did you last discuss their wants and needs informally?
   - Have you made any compromises to support them (juggled priorities to let them go on training events/holidays, etc)?

2 **I trust my boss; he/she is honest with me**.
   - Do your staff really know how you rate them?
   - Do your staff know your personal and business priorities?

3 **I know where we are going and how to get there**.
   - Ask your staff to lay out the top three priorities for the next three, six or 12 months. Are they the same as your priorities?

4 **I am doing a worthwhile job**.
   - Are you delegating meaningful projects, or just administrivia?
   - Are your staff clearly stretched, are they cruising in their comfort zone or are they grumbling about meaningless chores?

5 **I am recognized for my contribution**.
   - When was the last time you praised your team in public?
   - Do you let them star in front of senior management and other departments, or do you take the lead on all the big meetings?

When was the last time you praised your team in public?

06
Coaching

Purpose

The art of coaching is about helping people discover their own potential and resolve their own issues. It is not about telling them what to do or solving all their problems for them.

As a manager, you have a range of possible actions:

- instructing, telling and solving problems;
- giving advice and guidance, and suggesting ideas;
- giving feedback to people;
- asking questions to understand the context;
- looking for options;
- listening, summarizing and reflecting.

The basic idea is to gravitate towards the bottom of the list. For a coach, solving problems for people is a fatal mistake. It is attractive because:

- You get to look smart.
- The other person is happy because you have made life easy for him or her.
- You become more popular.

In the short term, this is attractive. In the longer term it is the road to ruin because the more you solve problems for people, the more they will bring their problems to you. You will end up with the problems of the world on your shoulders. Also, you are not letting your staff develop; the only way they will grow is if they climb their own mountains. You can guide, support and encourage them, but you cannot climb the mountain for them.

Gravitating towards the bottom of the list is hard work. Listening, summarizing and reflecting take time. And it is extremely frustrating when you know the answer and your team member is struggling to find it. You may develop blood blisters on your tongue from trying to avoid blurting out the answer. But the time invested in helping the other person discover the answer pays big dividends. You can help people become better team players so that they can start taking problems from you, rather than bringing problems to you.

There is one risk of coaching and letting your team members come up with a solution: they may come up with a better solution than the one you had thought of. Fortunately, the coaching method means that you will not have exposed your half-baked idea to them. Instead you can nod sagely at their great idea and let them proceed. As the leader, you take responsibility for the success or failure of the team, so letting them come up with the smart ideas is 100 per cent in your interests.

EXERCISE 3.7 Coaching

A colleague and friend from another department seeks your advice. You know she has been looking unhappy. Now she says she has been offered another job at a competitor. She asks you: 'In my shoes, would you take the job?' What are the questions you would ask to help her make up her own mind?

The more you solve problems for people, the
more they will bring their problems to you.

Structure

A good coaching session has a structure. Typically there are five steps, which can be thought of as the five Os: objectives, overview, options, obstacles and outcome:

1 **Objectives:** 'What do you want to focus on/achieve/review today?'

2 **Overview:**
   - 'Why is this important to you now?'
   - 'What is the situation?'
   - 'How do the other people see the situation?'
   - 'How do you know that?'
   - 'What do you/others feel about the situation?'
   - 'What are the potential consequences of this?'

3 **Options:**
   - 'Have you seen anything similar before? What happened?'
   - 'What choices do you have? What do others want?'
   - 'What are the risks and benefits of each course of action?'

4 **Obstacles:**
   - 'What will prevent you from doing this?'
   - 'How will you overcome these obstacles?'

5 **Outcome:**
   - 'So what you are going to do next?'
   - 'Do you need any help or support?'

Notice that each element of the structure is based on open questions, not on giving answers. (See Section 5 of Part Five for more on open questions.) The other core technique is silence, often referred to as 'wait time'.

Wait time is very difficult to achieve. Many people feel uncomfortable with silence. But do not feel obliged to fill the air with your brilliance. You need to give space for the other person to think and reflect, especially the more introverted types who like to think before they speak. Give them time and the quality of discussion will rise.

EXERCISE 3.8   Coaching structure

Use the questions you have developed in Exercise 3.7 and the structure in this section to role-play the exercise outlined in Exercise 3.7 with a colleague. Alternatively, create your own role plays.

Using the colleague/friend from another department, the possibilities might include:

- 'I think my boss is fiddling expenses. Do I tell Accounts?'

- 'One member of my team is making no effort at all. I have tried everything. But he seems to have the confidence of my boss. What can I do?'

- 'My head of department insists I must go to a presentation next week. It is the day of my child's school play, which I missed last year. I had booked a holiday. What can I do?'

Many people feel uncomfortable with silence. But do not feel obliged to fill the air with your brilliance.

07
Valuing others: cultural intelligence

The role of leaders and managers is to make things happen through other people. In the past, managers used to be able to see and control other people. Now you have to make things happen through people you may not control, you may not see and you may not even like. Perhaps the most extreme version of this is when you work on a global team: your team members will come from a different time zone, different language and different culture. Leading a global team is extreme leadership: if you can lead a global team you can lead any team. So find a chance to work on such a team: you will build the skills and experience to help you for the rest of your career.

So how do you manage people who are not like you at all? You can use MBTI and the Style Compass (see previous sections) to help you understand them. But still they will behave in unexpected ways and there will be miscommunications: these often lead to loss of trust and a breakdown in team work. Working on a global team, you can learn all about the different cultures on your team. All of these activities will help you build knowledge about your team members. But knowledge is never enough: you need intelligence as well.

Instead of building cultural knowledge, focus on building cultural intelligence. If you do this well with a global team, you can do it even better with your local team. You will appear to be a leader who naturally reads people and understands them. There is a risk you could become a popular leader that people actually want to follow.

Here is how you can build cultural intelligence, which is also intelligence about people and about leadership:

- **Seek to understand, not judge.** Everyone is different. They do things differently not to annoy you, nor because they are malicious, unreliable or incompetent. Most people most of the time want to do well. They do things differently because that is how they think things should be done. Understand why they do things differently. There is a chance that their way is better, at least in the context in which they work. If you judge others by the way you work, you are making assumptions about what is best. You may know what is best in your area of work, but no one knows everything. Be humble enough to find out what works best elsewhere.

- **Use positive regard.** We all think we communicate well and suspect that others communicate poorly. If there is a misunderstanding, it is never our fault: it is always the other person's fault. Collectively, that is impossible. Most misunderstandings can be eliminated if we use positive regard. Positive regard is about having respect for other people and starting with the assumption that they mean well. On good days we all show positive regard for others. On good days we do the right things the right way. That does not count. The bad days are our moments of truth when we establish our reputations. On bad days it is easy to get angry, frustrated and annoyed. That just makes things worse. Use positive regard and work to a good solution.

- **Communicate well.** The best way to communicate is to shut up. If necessary, put duct tape over your mouth and force yourself to listen. The more you listen, the more you understand. When you really understand what the other person is thinking, then you can influence them positively. Listening also pays them respect. They feel valued and will believe that they have been heard. Once they believe that they have been heard, they will be ready to listen. The best way to get other people to shut up and listen is to shut up and listen yourself. Don't talk over them: you just land up in a shouting match.

- **Learn and adapt.** Google is full of knowledge, of variable reliability. But it is devoid of intelligence. Knowledge is about know-what, intelligence is about know-how. Knowing what you need to do is often easy; knowing how to make it happen is harder. Working with other cultures and other people you can never amass enough knowledge to succeed. And that is pointless anyway: you are a leader, not an anthropologist. Your job is to observe, understand and then adapt quickly to all the signals that you are seeing and hearing.

These ways of thinking will help you in the extremes of leading a global team. They are also the basics of leading any team.

> The best way to communicate is to shut up.

08
Managing expectations

Managing expectations upwards

Expectations management is the lifeblood of corporate failure and success. There are three versions of the expectations game:

1 **The boss game.** The boss wants to set the toughest expectations possible. If you can deliver against high expectations, that eases pressure on the boss to deliver in other areas.

2 **The team game.** The team wants to have the lowest possible goals so that they can be achieved with the minimum of effort and risk.

3 **The handover game.** A departing manager will bequeath to the incoming manager a rosy picture of imminent success. If the incoming manager accepts this, he or she is dead meat: success will be put down to the work of the departing manager, and failure will be because the incoming manager is incompetent. Consequently, the incoming manager will rewrite history fast to paint a picture of imminent catastrophe. In this version of reality, the incoming manager cannot lose: if disaster strikes then it was the fault of the departing manager; if success happens, it is because of the heroism of the incoming manager.

This is not a game just for politicking middle managers. Look at how often profit warnings follow the appointment of a new CEO: the new CEO then makes a series of exceptional charges and write-offs to correct the failings of the previous CEO.

This is not always an uplifting game to play, but it is essential to survival. There are two golden rules to playing it well: play it hard and play it fast.

1 Play it hard. Anchor the debate on the most extreme case you can justify, and then marshal as much hard evidence as you can to justify your position. You will be negotiated down from the extreme position: this will show flexibility on your part while still enabling you to chase a reasonable goal.

2 Play it fast. Set expectations as early as you can. The later you leave things, the harder it becomes to change. If a top-down planning assumption of 20 per cent growth is made, you will find it hard to anchor the discussion on zero growth. If you have been in a post for two months, everyone will assume you will deliver on the targets your predecessor left you. Challenge and change expectations early.

> Challenge and change expectations early.

Idleness and success: a case example

Paul was about the idlest person in the office. But he always got the best bonus, and all the top management thought he was a great leader and produced wonderful results. He only seemed to work really hard for about one month a year. This was deeply irritating to the rest of us who worked hard all year for a lot less money and even less praise.

The one month Paul really worked hard was during the budget cycle. He would start setting expectations very early in the cycle. He would show how his part of the market was falling off a cliff-edge in terms of customer demand; he would prove that the competition was investing heavily. He would prophesy, Cassandra-like, the imminent collapse of civilization, or more specifically of profits. He would play hardball over this and overwhelm people with data to show he was right.

By the end of the budget cycle, he would be committed to a very low profit target. He would also have secured a large increase in resources to fight off the competition. He would then, heroically and against all the apparent odds, overachieve against the profit goal (even though it was lower than the previous year's goal). For this great achievement, he would get a great bonus. The rest of us, who had boldly accepted the stretching and challenging targets that management wanted to impose, would struggle all year to hit target and achieve a modest bonus.

Managing expectations downwards

Managing expectations downwards is nearly the mirror image of managing upwards. An effective leader needs to be unreasonable, selectively. In setting expectations, the leader learns to be selectively deaf: you will not hear all the excuses about rising input costs, increasing competition and demanding customers. You will stretch the team as far as it can go. This is important because people tend to rise or fall to the level of expectations set for them.

In schools, the power of expectation-setting is well established: expect kids to succeed and they will do well. Expect them to fail and they will fulfil your expectations completely. In this respect, business people are like schoolchildren: they rise or fall to the standard expected.

Effective expectations management is not only about setting expectations at the right level. It is also about setting the right psychological contract between the leader and the team member. The psychological contract has various elements on the leader's side and on the team member's side.

The leader's side of the contract is:

- Deliver bonus and promotion promises if performance justifies doing so.

- Give political support for dealing with other departments.

- Be clear about what working style works best in the team.

- Demonstrate an interest in and commitment to the future of each team member.

- Delegate effectively: give interesting opportunities, not just administrivia.

- Provide appropriate coaching.

The team member's side of the contract is:

- Deliver the results promised.

- Be 100 per cent loyal to and supportive of the leader.

- Work in an appropriate style for the current leader and team.

- Avoid surprises.

- Don't whine and undermine the morale of the team.

Within these very broad expectations there is a huge amount to be discussed. What are the right goals? What is the right working style? What is the best mix of assignments? Leaders cannot expect their team members to be telepathic: it helps to set these expectations explicitly. The expectations need to be discussed, not mandated. If team members feel involved in agreeing and setting expectations, they are much more likely to feel committed to them than to arbitrary expectations set from on high. Expectations setting should always be a two-way process.

> An effective leader needs to be unreasonable, selectively.

09
Managing performance

All firms have a performance management system, which is normally full of TLAs (three letter abbreviations) such as KPI, PDP, MBO. Despite the alphabet soup, most firms are lousy at managing performance, to the extent that leading blue chip firms have given up on annual appraisals. They are exercises in evasion and dishonesty, on all sides. However much we believe in performance, as human beings we do not like giving bad news to other people. And the annual appraisal is a demeaning exercise in which the hierarchy becomes a parent/teacher–child relationship. The boss acts like a teacher giving an end of term report to a child, who may be older than the boss. It is a mess. And yet, you have to manage performance.

Managing performance is not just about systems. It is about how you think: if you think about performance management the right way then it is easy, whatever the corporate system may be. Here are three ways to think differently about managing performance.

Focus on the future, not the past

There is limited value in telling people that they were good or bad boys and girls in the past. Instead, focus on what needs to happen in the future. This is not just about deadlines and outcomes. It is also an adult-to-adult discussion about what support and help they will need to succeed. This has to be tough conversation in which there are clear commitments. If those commitments are missed, that leads to another discussion about how to get back on track. If every commitment is consistently missed, that leads to another sort of discussion about where someone might best succeed, given they do not succeed in their existing role. But at least these are constructive discussions about working towards a better future.

Focus on development, not performance

Let's imagine you have just promoted a high flier. In their new role you give them 1/5 for performance: watch them throw their toys out of the pram as they have a tantrum. Now replay the same scene, where you measure development instead of performance. You promote the high flier and say that they are now at stage 1 of 5 in five stages of development in their new role. You are no longer insulting them. You are starting a conversation about how you can help them develop and go through all the development stages required to master their new role. The score is the same, but the outcome is totally different. Once you understand the skills and experience needed to master a role, you can move to a development framework which allows people to progress and learn. If you focus just on performance, you give people no incentive to learn: they just want to maximize performance today using the skills they have today. You can drive performance better by focusing on development, not performance, because you grow your team.

Focus on the journey, not the event

Performance reviews are often set piece events which are dreaded by both sides. So why not scrap them, like many top firms have done? Instead of one big set piece event a year, make sure you have regular conversations about development and progress with each team member. This means that feedback can be given in real time, and at the right time instead of coming as a surprise at the end of the year.

Inevitably, corporate systems will require that you fill in bits of paper and tick boxes in the right place so that HR can be kept happy. But if you are having regular conversations with each team member, you can turn this into a formality. Make the process transparent and invite each team member to help you fill in all the boxes. You want your team members to feel part of a team, which means treating them as adults and equals, so treat them that way. This may not make HR happy, but that does not matter. You need to look after your team, not look after HR.

> You can drive performance better by focusing on development.

10
Managing professionals

The chances are that you are a professional, so you should know how you would like to be managed. As an exercise, note down the five things you would most like from your boss in how you are managed. And now do the same things to your team members. Remember the golden rule: 'Treat others as you want to be treated.'

Professionals can be high maintenance: they can achieve much but they demand much. They have ambition and ego to match their ability and work ethic. And it's likely that they do not respect you: your team probably thinks they could do your job far better than you are doing. So how do you manage egomaniacs who do not respect you? In essence, professionals want less management and more leadership.

Here are the basics of managing professionals:

- **Stretch them.** Professionals are natural overachievers. Let them overachieve, learn and grow. An idle professional is a dangerous professional.

- **Set a direction.** Professionals do not respect weak managers: set a direction, be clear about how you will get there and stick to it.

- **Shield your team.** Focus your team on where they can make a difference. Shield them from the politics, routine rubbish and noise of corporate life. They may even be grateful to you if you do this well.

- **Support your team.** Set the team up for success: make sure they have the right resources, right support and right goals.

- **Show you care.** Invest time in each team member: understand their needs and expectations. Help them on their career journey.

- **No surprises.** Don't surprise your team at appraisal time: all trust will be lost. Have difficult performance conversations early so they can change course.

- **Recognize them.** Professionals have pride. Feed their egos: praise good work in public. Never, ever, demean them in public. Have the hard conversations in private.

- **Delegate.** If in doubt, delegate everything. Do not let them delegate problems back up to you. Coach them to solve the problem themselves: they will learn and be more valuable team members as a result.

- **Set expectations.** Some professionals want it all and want it now. Some want more and sooner. Any half-comment about bonus and promotion will be taken as a 100 per cent firm promise. Be clear and consistent in your messaging.

- **Manage less.** Trust your team. Manage by walking away. Micromanaging shows lack of trust and builds resentment among professionals. Trust your team and they will rise to the challenge.

Treat others as you want to be treated.

Part Four
Moment of truth skills

01
Taking control

Just because you have been made the boss, it does not mean you are in control.

Plenty of people confuse position with power. Even prime ministers can make this mistake. John Major, when prime minister, was attacked by his own colleagues for 'being in office, not in power'. It is very easy to get the big title and to then drift. The drifters are easy to spot: they accept the status quo they inherited. Of course, they will make the odd incremental improvement; they will fight the odd fire. But they will not make a fundamental difference, they will not take a risk and they will not be remembered. So if you want an easy life that is the way to go. If you want to lead, you have to take control and make a difference. And you have to move fast: within one or two months everyone will have made their mind up about you and it will be hard for you to change things.

Good leaders normally have a simple agenda, which boils down to three things: idea, people, money, or the IPM agenda:

1 **Idea.** You need to have a simple idea about what you will do that will be different from and better than the past. You can call this a strategy or a vision if you want to be grand. But it should be a simple idea which your team, colleagues and bosses can remember. The best ideas are simplest: 'We will increase customer satisfaction', 'We will increase reliability', 'We will reduce costs'. And make sure you set expectations well. Get all the skeletons out of the cupboard fast, so you cannot be blamed for them. Reset expectations as low as possible: it is easier to beat a low target than a high one.

2 People. If you have the B team, you have a recipe for sleepless nights and stress. Do not assume that the team you inherited is the team you must live with. Mould the team to the task, and make sure you get the A team. In some organizations you will be expected to act within weeks; in others it may take months to reshape the team. Do what it takes to move people on and bring the right people in.

3 Money. Make sure you have the right budget to fulfil your goals. And make sure the budget you have is being spent the right way: be bold in reshaping your budget to meet your aims. Again, never assume that what you have inherited is what you must live with. If you have been dealt a bad hand, it is your job to make sure you get a better one.

At a simple level, expect to work overtime when you first take over. You will be learning a new job, doing the new job and then reshaping the work and the team. And you will probably find that you will have to spend a disproportionate amount of time meeting and talking to people: your team members, colleagues and bosses. Invest time especially with your team: they will be nervous about their new boss. This is your chance to set a new psychological contract with them. Show how you will look after them (and be realistic about expectations) and show what you expect in return.

> If you want to lead, you have to take control
> and make a difference.

02
Conflict management

Principles

Organizations are set up for conflict. This is a surprise to most people, who think that organizations are meant to be as cooperative as bees in a beehive. So let's emphasize the point: *Organizations are set up for conflict.*

Different functions, business units and geographies will have different priorities. Internal conflict, be it nice or nasty, is how these conflicting priorities are resolved. Conflict is good, provided it is contained. Unconstrained conflict and open warfare are not good. The question is how leaders deal with conflict when it arises.

The first principle of conflict management is: do not take it personally, especially when it is meant to be personal. If you sink into the gutter in personal battles it does not matter if you win or lose: you will still smell awful. Stay aloof from the gutter and at worst you will get your ankles splattered. This is easy to say but hard to do. We need a simple tool that we can deploy in a conflict emergency. Welcome to turning the FEAR of conflict into the EAR of consensus.

Let's start with nasty conflict that feels highly personalized. The natural reaction is fight or flight: punching the CEO or running away is not good tactics. But the fear is real: we have to deal with it. Take the F out of FEAR (the bad response) and you are left with EAR (the good response).

FEAR stands for:

*F*ight furiously.

*E*ngage the enemy emotionally.

*A*rgue against all-comers.

*R*etaliate, and repudiate reason.

This can be fun, especially on your final day at work. It is also very common and very unproductive: it invites an intellectual, political and emotional punch-up.

EAR stands for:

*E*mpathize.

*A*gree the problem.

*R*esolve the way forward.

In the heat of battle, this is much harder and much more productive.

> Organizations are set up for conflict.

Practice

So how do you put your EAR into practice?

Empathize

Do not hug the other person. This might be misunderstood. Listen past the bluster and blame. Listen past the emotion. Let the person talk. Listen actively to show that you understand. (Look at the listening skills in Part Five, Section 5.)

Let the person blow off steam and cool down. Make sure you really understand his or her situation. Do not try to put your own point of view forward or justify yourself: it will only cause more conflict. Do not try to fight emotions with logic. Don't enter the other person's personal space: step back and give him or her time to cool off.

Agree the problem

Try to focus on the actions, outcomes and benefits desired. Do not do this until both of you are breathing normally and not shouting. When have you had sustained success from shouting at other people? This is where you move from listening and paraphrasing to asking questions:

'So what we need to achieve is...?'

'So where do we need to get to by next week/month?'

'What does the customer want as a solution?'

Resolve the way forward

Curiously, this is often the easiest part. Once you have all calmed down and agreed the situation and the problem, the way forward is often clear, if painful. To help resolve the way forward:

- Generate options: do not get stuck with a single-point solution.

- Get the other person to suggest more than one idea.

- Formally agree the next steps: ask the other person to summarize and then confirm the way ahead in writing.

EXERCISE 4.1 Practising conflict management

Set up a role-play with a tolerant colleague. Try getting really angry and shouting at your colleague. As a courtesy, let the colleague do the same to you. In both cases the 'victim' should just empathize. See which of you can sustain the anger longer. You will find it takes a huge amount of energy to sustain anger. It is emotionally draining. Anger pretty quickly blows itself out if it is met with the damp sponge of empathy.

As a second exercise, see what happens if the 'victim' starts to retaliate. Do not do this for too long, because emotions can get pretty high. Anger feeds on anger: soon you will both be in a shouting match.

It takes a huge amount of energy to sustain anger.

Tips of the trade

Beyond theory, there is reality. Here are some of the most common conflict management tips we hear suggested in workshops:

- **Become a fly on the wall.** Observe yourself: your language and your body. The fundamentals of this out-of-body approach to conflict call for Zen-like detachment. You do not have time to go to a monastery to master meditation so, in the short term, pretend you are a (smart) fly on the wall. Observe the emotion of the other person, but do not respond or get caught up in it. Imagine that it is a game: the goal is to manipulate the other person into calmness and agreement. It is easier to play a game where you know the rules than it is to fight a battle where you do not know the outcome.

- **Detach: how would someone else handle this?** We all have role models who do things very smoothly. Imagine you are your role model. What would he or she do next? How?

- **Escape to a happy land.** Everyone has a happy land in their heads to which they can escape at moments of idleness or stress. Go there. Chill out. Some people play games in their happy land where they can see the other person as a baby, or dressed in a tutu or being wiped out by a machine gun firing rotten eggs. It is quite difficult to get angry with a fat 50-year-old whom you see dressed in a tutu or as a baby throwing toys out of the pram.

- **Depersonalize: blame the situation, not the person.** When battles get personal, they get nasty. Instead of blaming someone for messing up, look at the context and circumstances that led to disaster. Perhaps there was not enough time or support, or there was lack of clarity about expectations. There are many reasons why things go wrong. Once you start this discussion, you defuse the emotion. You can start to deal with reality.

- **Buy time: it is hard to sustain anger.** If you follow the FEAR to EAR principles you will be buying time. As we have seen, it is tough to sustain anger. Let it vent. Then you can deal with reality.

> It is quite difficult to get angry with a fat 50-year-old whom you see dressed in a tutu or as a baby throwing toys out of the pram.

A radical alternative

Just occasionally, it is possible that we do something wrong. In many organizations, the standard operating procedure at this point is:

- Deny any wrongdoing: it has all been misinterpreted; that is not what happened.

- Spread the blame: you were told to do it or you were let down by someone else.

- Change the subject: in a superior way point out that we really should be focusing on more important issues, unless of course everyone wants to play the blame game....

- Shoot the messenger: this is mischievous gossip by rivals and others who are, as usual, up to no good and poisoning the well of corporate wellbeing.

- Under extreme circumstances, try a radical alternative: apologize. This needs courage and strength that few people have, and it needs to be done correctly.

The power of 'Sorry'

If you know you are in the wrong, it can be highly effective and unusual to say 'Sorry', which is a word that hardly exists in the corporate language. Be aware that when people are angry they are incapable of listening. You will often need to repeat the apology several times: this can be incredibly frustrating because it feels like people are rejecting you and your big gesture. In truth, they may not be able to listen past their emotions. Also, they will be picking up far more cues from your body language and tone of voice than from what you say. So if you start jabbing your finger at them and shouting 'Look, I've said sorry five times! Get it?' do not be surprised if their anger rises.

You will also need to act fast. Get your apology in early: the longer things are left to fester, the worse they become. People take positions, stories become exaggerated and a molehill becomes a mountain. Snuff the fire out before it spreads.

> Under extreme circumstances, try a radical alternative: apologize.

A sorry knight's tale

He had a knighthood, and he was very proud of it. He could bore for Britain on any subject, and he did. He thought a knighthood gave him the equivalent of papal infallibility.

In retrospect I was, perhaps, being marginally undiplomatic when I told him he was being arrogant and narrow-minded. The knight of the realm promptly exploded with pompous rage.

At this point, I was at decision time. I could deal with either reason or emotion. Dealing with reason I could have shown why I felt he was being arrogant and narrow-minded. But fighting emotion with reason is like fighting fire with petrol: it is not a smart idea. You have to fight emotion with emotion. We could deal with reality and reason another time. So I decided to say sorry. I had to say it eight times before he even heard it. This was painful. I felt like shouting at him for being so stupid and not listening and for ignoring my gesture of apology. I felt like giving him another sort of gesture altogether. But I kept calm, and then he calmed down.

He slowly realized he had been arrogant, narrow-minded and pompous while making a fool of himself in public. He spent the rest of the day apologizing to me. So I would then apologize to him (again) and everything was sweetness and light.

Saying sorry is never easy. But say it early, keep saying it, keep your cool and even the most pompous and cloth-eared knight will get the message. Of course, the real message should be to avoid getting into situations like that in the first place. But life would then be very tedious. And sometimes it pays to stand up to people (see Sections 4 and 7, Part Four).

Fighting emotion with reason is like fighting fire with petrol.

03
Crisis management

I t can't happen to us. Disasters are what happen to other people. Muggings, murders and mayhem belong to a different world from our nice, rational and safe world. And then it happens, and you are the leader.

You are at a conference in a different time zone. A panic phone call wakes you up at 2.30 am in your hotel room. What should we do? The press are on to us; the board want to know what is happening; friends and relatives are clamouring for information; everything is moving fast. Is the situation under control? Hell, no – that's why we called you: you're the leader. Tell us what we do – now. This is what the textbooks euphemistically call a 'moment of truth'. You are about to be made or broken by what happens next.

Crisis management does not start with the crisis. It starts long before. Recognize that it is not a question of *if* a crisis will happen, but what, where, when and why it will happen.

There is a three-part way of dealing with crises:

1 prevention;
2 preparation and practice;
3 prompt, professional, positive and proactive response.

Prevention

The best way to handle a crisis is to prevent it. Do a risk audit with your team. What are all the things that can go wrong? Work out the major categories:

- **legal**: employment, discrimination, product liability, confidentiality;
- **criminal**: fraud, theft, terrorism, violence, denial-of-service attack;
- **health and safety**: working practices, product contamination and scares;
- **technical**: data loss, power loss, water loss, website or IT systems crash;
- **operational**: loss of service, production, key staff;
- **financial**: bank covenants, takeover threat, receivables;
- **market**: loss of key contracts, customers, suppliers.

Find out what the major crises have been in the rest of the organization and in your peer-group organizations. This may mean that, like old generals, you find you are preparing to fight the last war. But it also means you are preparing against the most common and likely risks.

Preparation and practice

Prepare to respond not only to the known risks (above) but also to unknown and unplanned risks. You will not have time to prepare when the unexpected happens: you need to have a few preconditioned responses that will at least buy you some time until you can regain control of the situation. Preparation typically focuses on decision making and communication:

- **Decision-making clarity.** Be clear who has authority for releasing emergency spending and communicating to the media, staff, owners and customers.

- **Communication.** How will everyone communicate with each other? How will you find them in the middle of the night when no one is at the office? Who are the key people who need to come together to manage any crises: legal, PR, technical, HR, etc?

Take a little time to practise. Every organization does fire drills, although fire is one of the less likely disasters to strike. Prepare for other disasters as well: the whole of London's financial district goes through regular disaster recovery exercises. If a city can do it, so can an organization.

Prompt, professional, positive and proactive response

The Hitchhiker's Guide to the Galaxy has a very simple motto: 'Don't panic.' That could also be the motto for dealing with crises. This is difficult to do under stress and when everyone else is in a panic. But there are some common themes to handling crises from the minor to the major:

- **Prompt response.** A fast response is needed to provide reassurance that everything is being done to solve the crisis as fast as possible. This neutral response is about buying time while finding out what is really happening and regaining control. In the first stages of a crisis, emotional reassurance is as important as a logical response. This may not buy much time, but it helps.

- **Professional response.** People will judge you by how you appear and act as much as by what you say. If you appear calm, collected and committed, they will respond better than if you look panicky.

- **Positive response.** The leader needs to avoid letting the organization get into buck passing and playing the blame game. Make the team focus on discovering what they can do collectively to regain control and move forward. In the process of doing this, they are also likely to find out the root cause of what went wrong: it is hard to regain control without knowing why control was lost in the first place. However, you can leave the inquests for later.

- **Proactive response.** Your task is to come up with the plan as fast as possible. It will inevitably change as events unfold. This is unimportant: as long as people have some sort of plan to work to, they can make progress. Morale will rise simply by virtue of feeling that there is direction, there is a possible solution and they are making progress. If 50 per cent of the initial effort is wasted because the plan was not perfect, then be happy that 50 per cent of the effort was making a difference. As things become clearer, so you can focus and refine the effort.

Don't panic.

04
Dealing with bullies

It is very fashionable, in a post-modernist way, to avoid criticizing personal styles of management. It may be fashionable and post-modern, but it is also wrong. Here we will look at just two examples of destructive leadership styles: aggressive and passive.

Aggressive leaders fancy themselves as superheroes. The conference circuit and bookshops are full of these superhero stories. Aggressive superheroes think that only they can save the day because everyone else is too lazy or stupid. The results are:

- a demoralized organization, which many people leave;

- no effective succession, because such leaders have not given anyone the opportunity to grow: this leads to failure when they leave, proving to them that only they were saving the ship from disaster;

- a high dependency on the success or failure of one individual: in the United States, quite a few heroes are now in the tender care of the district attorney.

Passive people are unlikely to become leaders, unless Daddy owns the firm. They set up themselves and the organization for failure. Although they are not to be found at the tops of organizations, there are plenty of passive people lower down. As leaders, we have to work with both passive and aggressive types of person.

The ideal way forward is assertive leadership: this is positive, professional and proactive. It enables everyone to win, not just one person (see Table 4.1). The essence of the assertive leadership style is:

Table 4.1 Personal styles

	Passive	Assertive	Aggressive
Characteristics	Allow others to choose for you; inhibited; set up to lose.	Choose for self; honest; self-respecting; win/win.	Choose for others; tactless; self-enhancing; play to win.
Your own feelings	Anxious, ignored, manipulated.	Confident, self-respecting; goal-focused.	Superior, deprecatory, controlling.
How you make others feel	Guilty or superior; frustrated with you.	Valued and respected.	Humiliated and resentful.
How you are seen	Lack of respect; do not know where you stand.	Respect; know where you stand.	Vengeful, fearful, angry, distrustful.
Outcome	Lose at your expense.	Negotiated win/win.	You win at others' expense.

- Be clear about your agenda and needs.
- Explain, not tell; persuade, not order.
- Understand and respect others' needs.
- Balance active listening with talking.
- Set up win/win outcomes, not win/lose.

Against an aggressive bully it takes nerve to maintain the assertive style. Success depends on:

- **Preparation.** Know exactly what your interests are. Most of the time you can avoid a fight either by conceding things that are not important to you or by doing a judo throw: finding a way of aligning your interests with the bully's so that you work together, not against each other.

- **Professionalism.** Do not rise to the bait and fight: the bully will enjoy that far too much. If you fight, the bully will have to be seen to win and make you be seen to lose, otherwise the bully's self-perception will be destroyed. It will be a nasty fight, and the bully has far more experience of fighting like that than you do.

- **Practice.** Once you get used to it, dealing with bullies becomes a game to enjoy. You can observe their antics with a level of detachment and respond appropriately. Bullies know when they are wasting their time: they will go in search of an easier victim.

With a passive person the challenge is reversed. Instead of needing to take heat and energy out of the system, the assertive leader needs to *inject* some heat and energy. This goes back to the fundamental motivation skills in Section 5 of Part Three, which looks at how you can find the triggers that will activate each individual.

> Aggressive superheroes think that only they can save the day because everyone else is too lazy or stupid.

05
Negative feedback

The SPIN model

No one likes giving or receiving negative feedback. But not telling someone he or she is failing to meet expectations perpetuates the problem, misleads the individual and will create a crisis of trust and performance later. So deal with it promptly and give the person a way forward. Do this well, and you will build trust and respect.

SPIN – situation and specifics, personal impact, insight and inquiry, and next steps – is a classic and simple framework for giving negative feedback:

- **Situation and specifics.** Give feedback in the right situation: when the person is calm and the event is still fresh in the mind. Do not give feedback when people are angry, stressed, upset or very busy. When you give feedback, be specific about your purpose (Why are you doing this?), the circumstances and the event.

- **Personal impact.** Do not judge the other person: that invites conflict. Say how his or her actions made you feel: feelings are irrefutable. For example, say: 'You have turned up late to three client meetings; it makes me feel you think they are unimportant', not: 'You are a lazy idler', 'I was very embarrassed when the CFO saw the errors in the budget you prepared', or 'You are an innumerate scumbag.'

- **Insight and inquiry.** Ask questions to see if the person understands the problem, to help him or her explore and evaluate options and discover the way forward. Avoid telling people: make them learn for themselves.

- **Next steps.** Mutually agree what happens next. There needs to be a positive way forward. You need to have thought through possible options and actions. At this point, it is often better to go into coaching mode (see Part Three, Section 6) and get the person to generate the options and the way forward. He or she may come up with a better and more relevant solution than yours. In any event, people will feel more committed to their solutions than they will to yours. Get the person to summarize the next steps. This is the best way to check for understanding: people can only summarize well if they have heard and understood well. The act of summarizing will also then consolidate their own thinking and they will remember the feedback much better and, it is to be hoped, positively. Follow up in writing to confirm the understanding.

> No one likes giving or receiving negative feedback.

SPIN in practice

Giving negative feedback is like coaching. It is about helping other people discover for themselves what they need to do. Like coaching, it is about asking the right sorts of questions. It is also important to adopt the right style. Table 4.2 gives a few pointers to success and failure.

Table 4.2 Finding the right style

Success	Failure
Specific feedback	Generalized feedback
Balance positive/negative comments	All negative
Actionable	Non-actionable
Deal with the problem	Attack the person
Asking, involving	Telling
Understand the situation	No understanding

Ultimately, there is little point in giving negative feedback unless you can drive to action. Once you have validated the problem, you need to find some way of resolving it. The feedback session will be much more positive and productive if it is couched in the language of 'development', 'finding a way forward' or 'putting in place the skills and behaviours required for success'. Each person will have language they prefer. It is best to use actionable, future-focused and positive language. Backward-looking and analytical language ('Let's see how you messed up') rarely helps.

EXERCISE 4.2   Giving negative feedback

Try any of these role-plays with a trusted colleague. Before starting each one, think about the following:

- How will you apply the SPIN model?
- What are the specifics you have observed and how have they affected you?
- What are the open questions you will ask?
- What are the next steps you would want to see?

Role-plays:

1 A client has complained that one of your team members has twice been late in delivering key reports.
2 Some of your team are complaining that another team member is too negative and drains morale and energy.
3 A high-flying team member is suddenly not delivering to the standard or timing you expect.

Help people discover for themselves what they need to do.

06
Fighting battles

The enemy within is often more deadly than the enemy at the gates. The competition may be laying siege, but at least they are still outside the town walls. Your colleagues have the means, the motive and the opportunity to slip the knife between your shoulder blades.

Sometimes, fighting is unavoidable. But take care. Sun Tzu in *The Art of War* advocated fighting under only three conditions, all of which must be present: 1) only fight when there is a prize worth fighting for; 2) only fight when you know you will win; and 3) only fight when there is no alternative.

1 **Only fight when there is a prize worth fighting for.** Too many corporate battles are fought over trivia. If there is a trivial battle being fought, step aside and let others cover themselves in mud. If necessary, be noble and make a concession. You will now have earned some credit, and someone will owe you a favour.

2 **Only fight when you know you will win.** On Wall Street, if you don't know who the fall guy is, you are. If you must fight, win. A dead hero is still dead. Most battles are won and lost before the opening shot is fired: make sure you have the political support and ammunition to win before fighting.

3 **Only fight when there is no alternative.** It is better to win a friend than it is to win an argument. If you win an argument and make an enemy, the enemy will still remember you long after the argument has been forgotten.

Inevitably, there is an alternative strategy, which was advocated by Lord Nelson in his many battles against France and its allies: 'Any captain of mine who lays his ship alongside that of the enemy can do no wrong.' This ultra-aggressive doctrine would, on occasion, have small British ships attacking French battleships. The French knew they would have to fight if they went to sea, so they stayed in port where their fighting capabilities deteriorated fast.

> The enemy within is often more deadly
> than the enemy at the gates.

The Nelson doctrine is much used by entrepreneurs and a breed of self-styled hero leaders. When it works, it is highly effective and the leader is destined for the cover of *Fortune* magazine. For every successful hero leader, there are the corpses of thousands of dead would-be heroes.

> If you don't know who the fall guy is, you are.

It's your life; you decide.

> It is better to win a friend than it is to win an argument.

07
Power

In theory, smart and nice managers get to the top. You need to be smart (high IQ) and nice (high EQ or emotional quotient) so that you can deal with problems and people equally well. In theory there should not be war, famine or Morris dancing.

Now look at reality. Look at who succeeds in your own organization. The chances are that there are plenty of smart and nice people who have left or have been sidelined. Meanwhile, people who are not so smart or nice mysteriously levitate to the top of the organization. Being smart and nice may help, but clearly something is missing. IQ and EQ are not enough. The 'something missing' is PQ, or political quotient.

PQ is the art of making things happen through people you do not control, which makes it a core skill for any flat organization. You only succeed by influencing colleagues, customers and suppliers. As with most things to do with leadership, PQ is something we can all learn, and we can all learn to do better. To build PQ this is what you must do:

- **Build trust.** Always deliver on your commitments; find common ground with your colleagues – common interests, needs and priorities; make it easy for your colleagues – remove risks and obstacles to them working with you.

- **Create loyal followers.** Show you are genuinely interested in each member of your team and their careers; understand their needs; manage their expectations; build trust by having difficult conversations positively and early; always deliver on your commitments to them.

- **Focus on outcomes.** Work to clear goals that have visibility and impact across the organization.

- **Take control.** Have a clear plan for your department; know what will be different as a result of your work; build the right team and get the right budget and support for your plan. Do not accept as sacrosanct the plan, team and budget that you inherit.

- **Pick your battles.** Only fight when there is a prize worth fighting for; only fight when you know you will win; only fight when there is no other way of achieving your goal.

- **Manage decisions.** Understand the rational decision (What is the best cost–risk–benefit trade-off?); manage the politics (What will the CEO and power brokers expect?) and the emotional decision (What do I feel most confident about and what will my team feel committed to?).

- **Act the part.** Act like other influential people in your organization; be positive, confident and assertive; act like a peer to senior staff, not like their bag carrier.

- **Be selectively unreasonable.** Dare to stretch yourself, your team and others; make a difference by going beyond business as usual and beyond the comfort zone: this lets you learn, make an impact and build influence.

- **Embrace ambiguity.** Crises and uncertainty are wonderful opportunities to make a mark, take control and fill the void of uncertainty and doubt which others create. Ambiguity lets leaders flourish.

- **Use it or lose it.** Control your destiny or someone else will; you only remain influential if you use your influence.

> Crises and uncertainty are wonderful
> opportunities to make a mark.

08
Managing adversity

Sometimes things can look very bleak indeed. All leaders have crises: even Churchill had his 'wilderness years' between the wars. That came to a 20-year stretch of adversity.

There are typically five stages of dealing with major adversity. These were identified by Elisabeth Kübler-Ross in her research on the process of dying (*On Death and Dying*, Touchstone, New York, 1969). They are often seen as the stages people go through in dealing with any major setback in life:

1 **Denial:** 'I can't be on the slippery slope (of real or corporate life). I'm a winner.'

2 **Anger:** 'Why me? It's not my fault. I don't deserve this.'

3 **Bargaining:** 'Is there a way out? If I do x or y, can I buy some time?'

4 **Depression:** Reality sets in, but in the gloom there seems to be no way forward.

5 **Acceptance:** 'I accept my fate and am ready to move on to another life.' At least in corporate life, this is where the leader takes control and starts the process of renewal: death in one corporate life is the prelude to rebirth in another life of leading in the corporate, public, voluntary or entrepreneurial worlds.

It helps to recognize these symptoms. If you feel them you are not abnormal: you are a human being suffering the normal reaction to loss and adversity.

From a leader's perspective, these are unhelpful reactions. Inaction, depression and seeking to blame people are not recipes for success or recovery. To recover you need to focus on the future:

- **Create some options.** Find some ways to success or recovery, in your current environment or another one.
- **Take control; be proactive.** Do not wait for others to control your destiny for you.
- **Find some balance.** Your current employer does not own your soul. Know what is important to you and focus on making that work.

Do not read Nietzsche; it will only make your adversity feel worse. But do remember the one useful thing he said: 'That which does not kill you makes you stronger.' Most leaders learn from experience and from adversity. Surviving adversity builds knowledge and resilience.

EXERCISE 4.3   Reviewing adversity

Review a big setback you have had:

- How did it feel against the five stages of dealing with adversity?
- How did you handle each stage?
- How could you have handled it better?

Keep this in mind next time you face a major setback: preparation makes you stronger.

To recover you need to focus on the future.

09
Knowing who to trust

This is the trust paradox: trust everyone and trust no one.

In the short term, you need to be able to trust people. If you do not trust your team, you cannot delegate to them. If you do not trust your colleagues, you cannot work with them. If you do not trust your suppliers, they cannot supply you. Trust is the invisible glue which holds a firm together.

In the long term, trust no one. Time and again, executives find themselves cruelly let down in moments of truth by colleagues whom they have known and trusted for years. When this happens, it is devastating. It can happen to you at any time.

To resolve the trust paradox, first we need to consider the trust equation. That helps us understand the paradox and shows how we can deal with it. This is the equation:

$$T = (V \times C)/R$$

The trust equation shows that trust (T) is a function of values alignment (V) and credibility (C) offset by risk (R): high risk means you need higher levels of trust to work together.

In the short term we can build alliances based on the trust equation, and that will help us make things happen. And the more we work with people, the more we tend to trust them. We understand them better, which builds values alignment and we build a track record of credibility. But this is where things start to go wrong: we assume that we can now rely on our allies permanently.

Note the words of Lord Palmerston, who was Prime Minister twice in the 19th century: 'We have no eternal allies, and we have no perpetual enemies. Our interests are eternal and perpetual, and those interests it is our duty to follow' (speech to the House of Commons, 1 March 1848). As with nations, so with executives. You have no permanent friends or allies; there are only permanent interests. At some point, your interests and their interests will go different ways simply because you are in different roles and have different priorities. At that point, the basis of trust between you evaporates. They will pursue their interests and you will be left feeling betrayed.

Feeling betrayed and upset is not a good use of time for a leader. You have to manage your alliances properly. This means:

- **Always focus on common interests**. You have to keep on reinvesting in your relationship. Make sure you understand how their interests are evolving. Do this well and you will get early warning of when their interests are diverging from yours. That is when you know you can no longer rely unconditionally on your ally: be prepared to be let down.

- **Never rely on one person**. It is useful to have a powerful sponsor in the firm. They can clear the way for you, help you with politics, nudge you towards the right assignments. But if you rely on them alone, you become highly vulnerable: if your sponsor slips, you fall; if your sponsor moves, you are abandoned. You need a network of support.

- **Always have a plan B**. If your ally does not help you when you need it, what will you do? When you are let down, it is often too late for you to take evasive action. Always prepare a back up plan, so that you can avoid disaster.

- **Never mistake friendship for trust**. If you like your colleagues, you are fortunate. Friendship helps at the margins, but at moments of truth self-interest prevails. Feeling betrayed by a colleague is bad; betrayal by a friend is worse. Enjoy the friendship, but be objective about how far you can rely on your friends to bail you out if it is not in their interests.

10
Stepping up

Mountaineers get altitude sickness when they climb too high. The same is true with executives. Some are promoted too far and too fast and cannot acclimatize fast enough to the heights they have reached. Others are too cautious and do not want to climb too high. Your challenge is to balance ambition and capability. Too much ambition and you get altitude sickness, too little ambition and you get stuck in the valley of underachievement.

Which of the two types of person describes you best:

- **Type A.** You believe you should go for the top job when you are about 50 per cent ready. You know that no one can be 100 per cent ready for the top job, and you have the confidence that you will learn on the job. The more you apply for senior roles, the more you will learn how to succeed in the application process. If you are turned down for a role, that simply shows that the firm has poor judgement and it has missed an opportunity.

- **Type B.** You believe that there is no point in going for the top job until you are at least 90 per cent ready. You know you will need to hit the ground running and make a good impression from day one. You will not have time to learn on the job. So you will keep on building your skills until you are ready to step up. If a firm rejects you, it is worth listening to their reasons so that you can learn from them and raise your game further before applying for another job.

If you are type A, you fit the male stereotype.[1] Put negatively, you are prepared to blag your way into the top job and then hope to learn as you go. If you are type B, you fit the female stereotype. Inevitably, type A people are more likely to emerge in top roles faster than type B people, even if they are not so well equipped for the top job.

The more senior you become, the harder you have to push for the next step. Early in your career, if you work hard and do well you will be promoted because every firm wants to encourage the next generation of leadership talent. But as your career progresses, there are fewer opportunities and there is more competition. Leadership is not given to you; you have to take it.

How quickly you seize leadership opportunities is your personal choice. But you have to make your luck and then take it. At junior levels it is clear what you have to do to succeed. As you progress clarity descends into a fog of uncertainty. The rules of survival and success are not clear at the top. You have to read the air and work out what you really need to do to succeed. Good leaders turn ambiguity into opportunity. You will wait in vain to be told what success looks like. Instead, work out how you can really make a difference to the firm, then build your claim to fame. Your claim to fame is your stepping stone to the top.

Stepping up is your first and most important leadership challenge. It requires all the leadership qualities of ambition, self-confidence, dealing with ambiguity and uncertainty, taking control and seizing the initiative. You can hope to get lucky and be appointed to a top role, but luck is not a strategy and hope is not a method. As a leader, you make your own luck find your own opportunities. Over to you.

> Leadership is not given to you; you have to take it.

---

[1] This is based on original research with Future Leaders, which looked at why men were routinely getting to headships in schools faster than their female peers. There were other reasons as well: conscious and unconscious sexism at work, and unequal division of labour at home.

Part Five
Daily skills

01
Reading

Of course, we all know how to read, write, talk and listen. Don't we? It's just that our colleagues write drivel, never listen properly, don't read our elegant prose and bore us to tears with their presentations.

We are all each other's colleagues...

Reading socially is different from reading for business. Reading socially, we want to have our heads filled with surprise, delight or shock. Reading for business we do not want our heads randomly filled with what the writer writes. We need to read with prejudice, to read with an agenda of our own so that we are not sidetracked by the internal logic and brilliance of the document in front of us.

Reading socially, we let the writer stay in control and lead us. Reading for business, the reader needs to stay in control. Being led by the writer is a recipe for being led astray.

EXERCISE 5.1   Reading (and meeting) with intent

Before reading a significant business document, take a moment to note down the following three things:

1 What is my point of view on the subject being discussed?
This helps you avoid being caught by its internal logic. With an established point of view, you will be able to dazzle your colleagues with perspectives that they had not thought about, because they had let themselves get caught by the internal logic of the paper in front of them.

2 **What topics do I expect to be covered?** This helps you spot the invisible: things that have been omitted. You can also think of this as: 'What questions would I want to ask and have answered?' You will now look brilliant as you spot the invisible: the gaps that the writers hoped you would not notice.

3 **What actions or coaching items do I want to pursue with the writer when I see them?** This allows you to create a proactive agenda rather than being caught in the writer's agenda. You will now appear like a wonderful, sage coach who is positive, constructive and helpful.

These questions can also be applied to meetings. With practice, you will become very good at it. You will be in danger of looking insightful and proactive: you will always seem to come up with insights, spot omissions and drive to action. It comes down to learning to read: read with prejudice, with an agenda and with preparation.

Reading socially is different from reading for business.

02
Writing

We can't all be Shakespeare, and we don't need to be. But we do need to be effective in how we write. The best editor I ever had beat five writing rules into me. I still fail, but at least I try....

Write for the reader

Who are you writing for and why? Ask yourself why the reader should want to read your document and what you expect the reader to do as a result of it. This is your critical first step from which you can decide the purpose of the document, its storyline and the essential content. If you are unclear for whom you are writing, you are likely to end up with an unclear document.

Where you are writing for a group of people, work out which ones are essential to you. There will be one or two decision makers whom you need to influence: focus your document on them rather than trying to please everyone. A focused document will be much more powerful than an amoeba-style document that lacks shape, direction, backbone or purpose.

Tell a story

What is the one headline you want the reader to remember? Construct a storyline to support the headline. Throw away all the verbiage that does not drive to the headline. This helps you achieve clarity and focus. Do not start with all the facts and data you have lovingly assembled at great personal effort and cost.

Start by asking: *What is the message I need to get across?* One message is enough, two only confuse people for whom your document is one of several hundred they will see during the week. The message is driven by who you are writing for (see above).

Then ask: *What is the minimum amount of information required to support the message?* What other information directly supports the message? All the other information can disappear into a nice fat appendix, which everyone will ignore, but it will reassure them that you have done lots of work.

Even if you are simply writing a regular report, this is still an opportunity to tell a story about what is happening in your business and what needs to happen next. Every document should have a purpose, and the purpose should be communicated through a story. Long after the data has been forgotten, the story will be remembered – if you have bothered to work out what the storyline is.

Keep it simple

Use short words and short sentences. Remember the witty ditty: 'When you write, keep it short: a dozen words at most per thought. Rats!' Writing short is far harder than writing long. As Churchill noted at the end of a long letter to his wife: 'I am sorry I wrote you such a long letter. I did not have time to write a short one.' If you have a clear storyline, you should be able to keep it short.

Make it active

The passive and impersonal do not make a document look businesslike: they make the document boring. Make it readable instead, if you want it to be read.

Support assertions with facts

If something is important, urgent or strategic, explain why it is important, urgent or strategic to your reader. Otherwise you invite the reader to argue: 'It may be important to you, but it's not to me.' And take care: one bad fact will make the reader distrust everything you write.

> **EXERCISE 5.2** Writing to be read
>
> Take the longest PowerPoint presentation you can find and reduce it to one headline of 10 words maximum. Then draft a story of up to 100 words for it. Then draft a new six-page PowerPoint presentation. See if the short or the long version has more impact.

We can't all be Shakespeare, and we don't need to be.

03
Presenting

Substance

We have all sat through tedious presentations where the presenter fills the air with nothing more than self-importance and incoherence. Let us not inflict the same fate on others when we present.

A simple starting point for presenting is to work on the writing skills to establish the story and content you want to cover. The ancient Greeks treated public speaking as an art form. For them, and for us, good speaking has three elements, namely logos, pathos and ethos:

1 **Logos or logic.** Good speakers quickly answer the question: 'Why should I, the listener, listen?' They then say what they are going to say, say it and conclude by saying that they have said it. Clear, simple, effective and 100 per cent free of bad jokes badly told. The logic is essential in the first minute: you have to establish why they should want to listen. What is the problem, opportunity or perspective that they need to hear from you?

2 **Ethos.** This answers the question 'Why do I believe this person?' Build credibility fast; use facts to support assertions. Borrow credibility by quoting people who have helped or supported what you are doing.

3 **Pathos.** This builds the emotional connection with the audience. Facts and logic are not enough. Tell a story and relate your message to their needs and their experience.

Building ethos, pathos and logos depends on knowing who you are talking to. The larger the group, the more mixed it is. In this case, figure out who you really want to influence. It is likely to be just one or two very important people. Focus your efforts on those people. It will make the entire presentation seem more focused and lively. It will also be more persuasive to those you want to persuade.

EXERCISE 5.3 Becoming a great Greek (and business) demagogue

Work out your logos, ethos and pathos for the following:

- Introduce your organization to an industry conference with 300 people present.

- Review what you have learnt about leadership with a group of 20 at a company away-day.

Logos, ethos and pathos.

Style

Style counts. Over 70 per cent of the information we absorb is visual. So if you are the king of the mumblers, dress like a tramp and slouch like a teenager in full hormonal angst, the brilliance of your message will be lost on the audience. Instead, focus on the three Es:

- energy;
- enthusiasm; and
- excitement.

Think of the worst presentation you have attended. Did it have the three above characteristics? Probably not. Here are some practical tips to help you.

Throw away the script

Reading from a script, you will sound wooden. Instead, memorize your opening to make a good start, and your conclusion to make a good finish. Memorize some choice phrases that you can insert on your way through: each phrase is a way-marker on your speech. You will keep your structure and discipline while sounding spontaneous.

Avoid complicated slide presentations

If you have slides, the principle is to have stupid slides but a smart presenter. The slide might have three or four key words to help the audience anchor where you are: you provide the commentary. The nightmare is to have smart slides that explain everything and a stupid presenter who reads the slides more slowly than the audience.

Stand tall

Stand on the front of your feet, so that a slip of paper could pass under your heel. Weight on the back of the foot encourages slouching and down energy.

Engage the audience

Look individuals in the eye, rather than gazing into the middle distance. Do not stare at one person the whole time. Get into a rhythm of using and completing one phrase or sentence while you look at one person and then move on to the next phrase and the next person in another part of the room. This has three valuable effects:

1 The audience will be electrified and pay attention when they all know they are likely to be engaged directly by you. Or put it the other way: if you appear to ignore them, do not be surprised that they appear to ignore you.

2 You stay very aware of how people are responding to you.

3 Your own energy levels will go up, you will appear very focused and the audience will respond with high energy and focus.

Rehearse

The more you rehearse, the more confident and comfortable you will feel. Even if you cannot rehearse everything, make sure you do the following minimum rehearsal:

● Rehearse the first 30 seconds intensely. When you start is when your nerves will be highest and everything can come out all wrong. But if you are word-perfect in the first 30 seconds, you will make a smooth and confident start, the audience will engage with you and you will have time to settle down.

● Rehearse the key phrases you want to use to make key points and to move from one part of the logic flow to the next. Work on the choice phrases: people will remember them long after they have forgotten everything else.

● Rehearse the last 30 seconds. 'Are there any questions?' is a feeble finish. Effective finishes often include a direct appeal to the audience, such as: 'I wish you all success on this great adventure we are now starting', 'I look forward to working with each one of you on this exciting initiative', or 'Each one of us can now leave a lasting legacy.'

The three Es are greatly enhanced by two more Es: expertise and enjoyment. If you are expert at your subject, you are more likely to relax and enjoy what you are saying. If you are enjoying it, your audience is likely to enjoy it as well. If you hate it, do not expect the audience to enjoy it.

EXERCISE 5.4 Presenting

Try telling someone about how the cost allocation system in your organization works. See if you fall asleep before your audience does.

Now try recounting one of the most memorable events in your career. You will naturally display all five Es: energy, enthusiasm, excitement, expertise and enjoyment. Such a simple exercise shows that we can all speak well: we simply have to transfer our skills on to the big stage.

Have stupid slides but a smart presenter, not the opposite.

04
Storytelling

EXERCISE 5.5 Simple storytelling exercise

Try this simple exercise:

- Recall and explain a spreadsheet from a month ago.
- Recall and give an account of a memo or e-mail from a month ago.
- Recall and retell a story you heard a month ago.

Normally, this exercise works. Do not, however, try it with a group of actuaries: you will spend the next three hours being told about spreadsheet disasters and triumphs. But back on planet earth, most earthlings find it far easier to recall a story than a spreadsheet or a memo. Presentations will be recalled only if they told a story, not for the brilliant words and numbers that the presenter slaved over for days and weeks.

Leaders understand the power of a story. A good story is memorable and has an emotional intensity that no amount of facts and argument can achieve. Most corporate stories talk about the journey we are taking, and the obstacles and opportunities that lie along the road. Effective leaders are often effective storytellers.

A good story has the following elements:

- Meaning and relevance to the listeners or readers: remember you are writing for the readers, not for yourself.

- A storyline, which will have:
  - A beginning, which is often framed as a challenge for the hero or organization to overcome. The resolution should not be clear from the start, otherwise all the suspense and interest are lost.
  - A journey, which tells how the challenge was or will be overcome.
  - An ending: a resolution in which there is often a lesson or a sudden insight or reversal of fortune. The best stories have an element of suspense and uncertainty.
  - Emotional impact: readers or listeners should be able to see themselves in the story, and should be able to see themselves overcoming the challenge presented.
  - Authenticity: the story should come from your heart so that it has your voice and your passion behind it.
- The story should relate to a reality that both storyteller and listeners recognize.

To see the power of stories in action, look at the stories chairmen and CEOs spin to the financial media. They tend to be captured in a few very simple headlines:

'We are entering a price war, so we are going to cut costs hard.'

'We need scale economies to drive down costs, so we will acquire other companies and integrate them.'

'No one is competing in the bottom end of the market, so we will enter it.'

'We will diversify our sources of income into less cyclical markets.'

'We are going to refocus on a few core businesses where we are leaders, and sell the other businesses.'

Each of these simplistic headlines may reflect months of work, and may well drive the efforts of the whole organization to success or failure. But they are very simple messages that most people can remember easily and act on.

Ivan's terrible day

Ivan was in despair. He had tried everything to show that a major change in strategy was required. He had charts and data and research in plenty of reports and PowerPoint presentations. The more he hammered away at his facts and figures, the more things went wrong: some people would nit-pick his data; others would simply switch off under the barrage of data. In his frustration he went to the flipchart and drew a picture.

'Look,' he said, 'we are on this side of the river. We are being attacked non-stop by competitors who are taking our territory. On the other side of the river there are these green pastures that no one has yet occupied. And the good news is there is the bridge to those green pastures if we can work with the right partners. We need to move now, before it is too late.'

There was a deafening silence. People looked at the picture. It might be possible to argue with some of the detailed numbers. But everyone knew in their hearts you could not argue against the big picture. The reality was staring them in the face: they knew they had to move. The meeting switched gear from analysis and denial to working out how to move across the bridge. From then onwards, crossing the bridge to the green pastures became part of the language of the organization.

EXERCISE 5.6   Telling the story of your journey

Develop a story that tells about the journey that you are taking your organization on. Work out how the story changes for your team members, for other departments and for the CEO. It helps to think about:

- What do they need to know about the journey?
- What might their role in the journey be?

Develop a story that talks about the journey you are on: are you on the right journey, or do you need to turn down another road?

A good story is memorable and has emotional intensity that no amount of facts and argument can achieve.

05
Listening

Listening is the leader's secret weapon. It is easy to tell people what to do, how to improve or how to solve their problem. But instead of telling, try asking and listening. Let them discover what to do and how to improve. Let them discover the answer to their problem. That way they have more ownership and commitment to the way forward, and they learn some skills and independence in the process.

There are three keys to effective listening:

1 **Paraphrasing.** When someone talks, try paraphrasing back to them what they said. If you get it right, the other person will be delighted that you were listening so well. If you get it wrong, you will quickly avoid any future misunderstandings. Paraphrasing is not the same as agreeing: it simply shows you have understood the other person.

2 **Asking open questions.** The more open the question, the more people talk. A closed question gets a yes or no answer. It gives little information and often leads to conflict. Open questions often start 'How would you...?', 'Why did they...?' or 'What would you do if...?' Closed questions often start 'Do you agree...?' or 'Shall we...?'

3 **Debriefing.** After any significant meeting, spend a few minutes debriefing with a colleague. You will both have heard and seen different things. Together, you will quickly get more intelligence and feedback than if you try scribbling notes furiously during the meeting. An effective debrief will cover the following:

– *Hot buttons*: What were the hot buttons for each person at the meeting? Did we press the hot buttons effectively and get people properly engaged with their issues? Did everyone have the same hot button or different ones?

- *Red issues*: What were some of the objections, issues and challenges people raised against what we were saying? Did we handle them? What do we do about them next?

- *Roles*: Who had what role in the meeting? Who is the real decision maker? Do they all have a common agenda or not?

- *Body language*: What was that telling us about how people were feeling about each of the topics that arose?

- *Our own performance*: How did we do? What could we do better both individually and as a team? How can we divide up responsibilities better next time?

- *Next steps*: What happens next and who is going to do it?

Listening judo

Chris is an expert at listening judo. He always has very strong opinions and he likes to get his way. He does so not by talking, but by listening. He is so smart that he knows the best thing to do is to shut up and listen at the start of a meeting.

When everyone has had their say, and largely cancelled each other out with their contradictory views, Chris will step in to offer a summary of what he has heard. He will then carefully extract a few half-formed ideas he has heard from each person. He will present them back to the group as the wonderful ideas that Kate, Julia, Jim and Amir had. As he does this, you can see Kate, Julia, Jim and Amir puff up with pride. Each person's idea has not only been heard in the babble of the meeting: it has been recognized as a smart idea and it is seen as that person's idea. Everyone is now eating out of Chris's hands. No one is going to argue against him, because that would be tantamount to arguing against their own ideas.

Naturally, Chris's summary just happens to support the prejudiced agenda that he entered the room with. By the end of his summary, the war is over. Chris has not only won the intellectual battle, but he has won friends all around the room.

Long after the meeting is over, Chris will still attribute all the great ideas not to himself but to others. As a result, he builds networks of deeply loyal colleagues and there is no chance that the ideas are going to get unpicked.

EXERCISE 5.7   Listening skills

Try paraphrasing, perhaps in a role-play with a colleague. After your colleague has spoken, summarize by saying 'So what you mean is...' or 'If I can summarize what you said...'.

Create a list of open and closed questions you can ask in different situations. Start by noting what sorts of questions other people ask and whether those questions get productive or unproductive answers.

Test your listening skills by doing debriefs with a colleague who has been to the same meeting as you. Ask the following:

- Who said what? (Who was in favour? Why? Who was against? Why?)

- How did people react at different stages (body language as well as words)?

- What did you learn about the agendas and priorities of each person present at the meeting?

Video yourself and focus on questioning. Make a T-chart. On one side, keep track of the number of open questions you ask. On the other, keep track of the closed questions. What sorts of responses do these elicit?

Listening is the leader's secret weapon.

06
Doing numbers

Managers use numbers the way drunks use lamp posts: for support, not illumination. We all know what the answer should be in the bottom right-hand corner of the spreadsheet. So we manipulate the assumptions until the correct number appears, with a bit of safety margin thrown in for good measure.

For the leader, reviewing a spreadsheet is not about the numbers: it is about the assumptions that lie behind the numbers. An effective leader has three ways of testing the numbers:

1 **Know your key data inside out.** You lead the business; you should know the key numbers and ratios. Do not get confused by the whole spreadsheet: look at the key numbers and ratios used and see if they fit with what you expected. If not, push hard to find out why.

2 **Play that 'What if...?' game.** You should know not just the key numbers and ratios, but all the key sensitivities in the business. They might be prices, market share, market growth, costs, interest rates or many other items. Ask what assumptions have been made and how the result would change if different assumptions were made on these sensitivities.

3 **Know who is presenting the numbers and why.** The credibility of the numbers is directly related to the credibility of the presenter. A cautious profit projection from an executive with a great track record is worth far more than an exciting profit projection from an untested executive. Turn this logic around for a moment: if you are the presenter, make sure you have credibility on your side. Get the support of the finance department and of seasoned and trusted executives before finally presenting your numbers.

The leader also needs to beware of the motives behind the numbers. When not using numbers like drunks using lamp posts, executives will use numbers like lawyers using facts. They will use the numbers selectively to make a point.

EXERCISE 5.8 The numbers (and assumptions) game

On a blank sheet of paper write down the key numbers and ratios for your business: financial, market and people numbers. Now compare them with the actual numbers. Draw up your key data list of the sacred and serious numbers and ratios you need. Learn them.

Play the numbers game. Look at a company budget or five-year plan: what are the key assumptions and how would you plausibly massage them to produce a huge profit or loss? What actions can you take to influence a positive outcome on the key assumptions?

Managers use numbers the way drunks use
lamp posts: for support, not illumination.

07
Problem solving

Answering the right question

The first rule of problem solving is: do not try to do it all by yourself. A solo answer is rarely better than the group answer. Even if it is a good solution, no one else will own it and you will have to spend excessive amounts of time getting others to accept your solution. Let them work on the problem with you and own the solution with you.

As a leader you will not, however, simply present other people with a problem. You will have thought it through sufficiently to know:

- You have the right problem.
- You are focused on causes, not symptoms.
- You know who needs to be involved in the solution because of their skills, interest or position in the organization.
- You have created some thought-through options.
- You have a structure or approach for solving the problem.

The critical step is to find the right problem. Three questions for you to ask about the stated problem are:

1 Who owns this problem? Who really wants this fixed?

2 What are the consequences of not fixing it?

3 What are the consequences of solving the problem?

If there are compelling answers to these questions, you probably have the right problem and you will quickly find out who are the right people to involve in solving it.

EXERCISE 5.9   Making sure you are solving the right problem

There are many good exercises to show how group problem solving is better than individual; go to www.wilderdom.com/games for a selection of exercises.

Look at your current projects and see how well they fare against these three questions:

1 Who owns this problem? Who really wants this fixed?
2 What are the consequences of not fixing it?
3 What are the consequences of solving the problem?

Find the right problem.

Process and techniques

Welcome to the world of fish bones, six thinking hats, brain-storming, synectics, SWOT, Pareto analysis, decision trees, metaplanning, mapping, Chicago rules, concept fans and many more problem-solving techniques. There are countless problem-solving resources available on the web, and many facilitators if you need them.

The basics of any problem-solving process are relatively straightforward:

- **Understand the problem.** Be clear who has the problem and the consequences of fixing it or not. Learn enough about the problem to know that you are focused on causes, not symptoms. Keep asking 'Why...?' to find out the root cause of the problem.

- **Create hypotheses.** Some people advocate complete brainstorming ('What if we covered New York with sticky treacle?'). But if you have really understood the problem, the answer is often not far away. To create insight as opposed to funky ideas, look at the problem from new angles. How do our customers see this? How will the competition exploit this? How has this been handled elsewhere in the world or in other industries?

- **Evaluate and select the best hypotheses.** Don't waste time evaluating every option. Let the group pick the two or three they most want to work on. The best ideas normally come through. If you are leading the group, you can use leader's rights to add one more for group consideration.

- **Drill down to action planning.** If the first three steps have been completed well, this is the easiest step. The drill-down may reveal further, lesser, problems, which can be solved with the same process.

Facilitation techniques

Here are some simple rules to follow in a brainstorming, problem-solving and team-building meeting. You should ask a facilitator to enforce the rules. Like a referee at a sports game, the facilitator must avoid taking sides. The facilitator's job is to enforce the rules. Some facilitators have a big book of rules, which just gets in the way of a productive discussion. At most, you need four rules. People can just about remember and respect four rules. No one will remember 50 rules, and you cannot follow what you cannot remember. The four rules are:

1 Benefits before concerns. Smart people like to show they are smart by showing they have analysed a problem and found its weaknesses. This is good survival strategy: we avoid doing stupid things. But it also means that we kill ideas before we know how good they are. It is far tougher, and more productive, to understand the benefits of an idea before we see the concerns.

2 **No heat-seeking missiles.** This is an extreme version of 'benefits before concerns'. Watch when an idea is shot down by a smart intellectual missile. Everyone quickly learns that having ideas is dangerous, so they shut up and that is the end of constructive thinking.

3 **Headlines before the detail.** Think of newspapers: a three- or four-word headline is all you need to understand the thrust of a story. Stop people giving long speeches: focus on getting ideas out. This makes the facilitator's job easier: it is possible to write headlines on a flipchart; it is not advisable to try writing speeches on one.

4 **Express concerns positively.** Instead of, 'That's stupid – it costs far too much', try, 'How can we improve the cost–benefit profile?' The first statement leads to conflict; the second to a productive discussion.

Like a good air traffic controller, a good facilitator will make sure that all the ideas that are raised land safely on the flipchart. When lots of ideas are flying, the facilitator will need to put some in a holding pattern until cleared for landing. A good facilitator will make this feel natural and productive to the group.

EXERCISE 5.10   Using the problem-solving process

Use this framework to discuss with a colleague any of the following:

- How would you reduce crime?
- How would you increase pensions?
- How would you increase savings?
- How would you beat the competition?

You cannot follow what you cannot remember.

08
Time management

Time management is not about being busy. We are all too busy already, and there is an infinite amount of work to be done. It is about being effective with what time we have. There are many tips and techniques, like:

- Handle each piece of paper or e-mail only once.
- Do it right first time.
- Keep a clear desk for a clear mind (and hope you do not have a wooden desk).

But let's make it simple. The following exercise, if put into practice, will make you more time-effective than most people.

> Keep a clear desk for a clear mind (and hope
> you do not have a wooden desk).

EXERCISE 5.11   Three ways to improve time
management

1 **Decide what you really want and need to do.** This is the old-fashioned list of goals and priorities for the year, the month, the week and the day. Clear goal focus makes it easier to know what not to do, what to delegate and time traps to avoid. A simple test of time well spent is to ask: 'How will I remember

this year in 20 years' time?' Rest assured, you will not remember this year for the number of e-mails you sent or the bonus you got. You will remember it for what you accomplished. If a year is too long to think about, then ask yourself: 'How will I remember this month at the end of the year?' You will not remember it for getting the expense report in on time, sending 620 e-mails and treading water.

2 **Find out what you actually do.** Keep an activity log for a few days. See how much relates to your priorities. Decide how much you can delegate, reduce or stop. If the 35-hour working week was really enforced, some people would have to spend at least 100 hours a week in the office to do 35 hours of work, after eliminating breaks, internet time, personal calls, gossip, wasted meetings, lunch, and planning the next holiday, office party or wedding.

3 **Create your prioritized to-do list for today, and follow it.** This should fall out of your goals list. ABC analysis (or red/yellow/ green) is a simple way to prioritize your time and tasks so that you deal with the A-list before the B-list before the C-list (if ever). There is a trade-off between what is important and what is urgent. Fundamentalist followers of Covey say you should only focus on what is important: but then when do the urgent things get done? And if only the important things get done, we would have cars with engines but without radios, heaters, power steering, side windows and any creature comforts. Equally, if you only do the urgent things, that is a recipe for being in a flat panic and firefighting all day. Ignore the rhetoric and theory from self-professed gurus: find a balance that works for you.

You will not remember this year for the number of e-mails you sent.

09
Hearing feedback

Discovering the truth

In most cultures, bosses do not like giving feedback, especially if it is negative. Like the jilted spouse who is the last to discover the truth, so the last person to hear about a performance problem is the owner of the problem.

In theory, you should be able to ask for feedback and you should get it. In theory, wars, famine and poverty should not happen. In practice, you need three strategies for finding out where you stand.

1 *Watch the feet, not the mouth: actions speak louder than words.* You will know how well you are doing by how far your boss entrusts more work, and more important work, to you. If you are being overloaded with highly demanding work, do not complain too loudly: this is a sign that the boss trusts you personally and values your ability to deliver results. If you find yourself with time to burn while all your colleagues are very busy, start to worry. Start asking for assignments: if you are met with evasive answers and prevarication then that is a sure sign the boss is not confident about you. You need to start finding some simple tasks where you can deliver, demonstrate your competence and build trust.

2 *Listen to the silence.* You know what the formal evaluation criteria are for your role. You should also understand the informal ones your boss will use. Listen carefully to any comments your boss makes and see which criteria he or she is talking about. Then listen very carefully indeed to what the boss is not saying. If the

boss praises you on five criteria and ignores another four, you should ask yourself (and your boss) why there is such silence on the missing topics. At best, the boss simply has no information about those areas: make sure you provide him or her with the evidence required. It may also be that the boss has some concerns. Find out about them early and you can do something about them.

3 *Be your own boss.* Evaluate yourself against these key benchmarks:

- How am I doing against the formal evaluation criteria?
- How am I doing against the informal evaluation criteria?
- How am I doing against the best of my peer group?

This is how the boss will think. If you have already thought this through you will at least be well prepared for the evaluation meeting with your boss. More to the point, you will be able to take action to make sure you are performing well.

> The last person to hear about a performance problem is the owner of the problem.

Listening through the pain barrier

When you are hearing feedback, it is very easy to hear badly. The three most common mistakes are as follows.

1 *Dr Pangloss's trap.* Voltaire's Dr Pangloss declared that 'Everything is for the best in the best of all possible worlds.' We like to hear good news, and at least some of us have cloth ears when it comes to bad news. The shrinks say that we are in denial. It can be painful to hear bad news, but it is important to hear it so that we can act on it.

2 *The Cassandra trap.* Cassandra did not actually say that 'everything is for the worst in the worst of all possible worlds', but she was still a pretty miserable companion. She was always foretelling doom and gloom. Sunny weather would, for Cassandra, simply be a prelude to a storm. Just as some people cannot hear bad news, so others only have to hear a marginally adverse comment to go into paroxysms of despair.

You need to hear both: build on strengths and find ways of working round weaknesses. Some bosses advise you to 'work on your weaknesses'. This is a recipe for disaster: no one succeeded by working on weaknesses. Like sports people, leaders do not focus on weakness: they focus on their strengths.

3. *The perceptions trap.* Perceptions may not be real, but their consequences are. The boss may be wrong to think that you are an idle layabout. The perception may be wrong, but the consequences of that perception will be very real.

When you hear bad news do not get defensive or aggressive. Try to listen objectively. Go back to some of the principles of coaching (Part Three, Section 6) and negative feedback (Part Four, Section 5). Make sure that you understand what is being said and then how you can jointly move to action:

- What is the issue we are talking about?

- What are the practical and specific examples of this issue? Is this an occasional and minor matter, or a regular and serious matter?

- What are some alternative strategies for dealing with the examples raised? How would the boss have dealt with those situations differently?

- How can we move forward?

- What coaching and training support is available?

- What does this say about the sorts of assignments I should take on?

- What are the practical next steps?

- When shall we meet again to review progress?

Make sure that you leave with a positive, and shared, agenda about how you will work together on the topics identified. Give the boss some stake in the game, through a coaching, training or assignment responsibility. And follow up: make it impossible emotionally, politically or rationally to return to the same negative issues at the next formal review meeting.

Perceptions may not be real, but their consequences are.

10
Using technology

It is possible that the major technology companies are in a conspiracy to destroy capitalism as we know it. Technology can be the single greatest destroyer of productivity in an office. For instance:

- **Presentations.** These used to be short and to the point, because they were hard to produce. PowerPoint allows anyone to create a vast presentation. This means that executives waste their time producing PowerPoint: if that is the best way they can use their time, they should be paid accordingly. Second, it means that presentations are too long, miss the point and waffle.

- **Communications.** E-mail is a curse, and 'reply all' is a plague. It is massively misused, mainly as a way of leaving an evidence trail to show that if it all goes wrong, it was not your fault. E-mails generate more e-mails as everyone feels the need to show they are helping. Instead of sending an e-mail, walk across the office and talk. Or even pick up the phone. No one ever built trust by sending e-mails, but teams depend on trust.

- **Social media, games and internet shopping.** These are all wonderful substitutes for work. Done well, you can make it look like you are working at your desk while wasting your time.

- **24/7.** Technology is the monster that has escaped the zoo and is out of control. Because we can be in touch 24/7, we feel we ought to be in touch. We may not actually be doing anything, but there is always the nagging feeling that maybe we should check e-mail one more time. The danger is that we never switch off.

Just as technology is the great destroyer, so it is also the great creator of productivity in the office. The problem is not technology, but how we use it. Just because we can use technology, it does not mean we should use it. If we take the four examples above, here is how you can make sure technology boosts your productivity rather than destroys it:

- **Presentations.** Good presentations are like diamonds: they benefit from good cutting. Reduce your presentation to your core message, and strip out everything else. The result will be shorter and better. If it is short enough, you can use PowerPoint yourself to produce the presentation. If you need fancy graphics or lots of appendices on a just-in-case basis, find an expert in PowerPoint to produce it for you: they will be better, faster and cheaper. If the most value you can add to your firm is producing PowerPoint slides, then take up that job at that pay rate.

- **Communications.** There is hierarchy of communication. Most effective is face-to-face: you can see people's reactions and you can adjust in real time. It is easy to build trust and avoid miscommunication. Then comes the phone: you cannot see the other person, but at least you can adjust to them in real time and hear their voice. Finally, there are the asynchronous forms of communication such as e-mail. These are fine for routine transactions and sending files, but not for discussion and debate.

- **Social media, games and internet shopping.** You can use these to enhance your productivity. Use all of these distractions as a reward for yourself. Set yourself a series of small targets, or tasks to complete during the day. Maybe you need to make a series of difficult phone calls: promise yourself a few minutes of social media time when you have completed a set number of calls. Combining rewards and short interval scheduling will encourage you to pick up the pace and complete tasks. It will also give you time to relax: every study for the last 100 years has shown that people perform better if they take a few minutes off every hour. Do not feel guilty about wasting five minutes an hour: make sure the other 55 minutes are genuinely productive.

● **24/7.** Leading firms are now seeing that the monster is out of control and are trying to tame it by introducing e-mail free days. Ultimately, it is up to you to control the monster. Decide when you will answer e-mails and stick to it: you can even put an auto-reply telling people when they can expect a reply from you.

Make sure that technology is your servant, not your master.

> No one ever built trust by sending e-mails.

Part Six
Organization skills

01
Making decisions

Rational, political and emotional decisions

If you believe economists, decision making is political. If you believe economists, you would not have predicted the last recession but you would have predicted 10 more since then. Decision making in firms is not just a rational exercise. It is also deeply political and emotional. A good decision works at all three levels.

Rational decision making

In theory this is where you can use decision trees, mind maps and Bayesian analysis. As a practising manager, you need a simpler way of thinking about decisions. At the heart of good business judgement is pattern recognition: once you have seen the same movie a few times you know what happens next and you can prepare accordingly. This is tough if you are new in the post: you will not have seen the movie before. So that is when you need to get help from people who have seen it all before. But you need to triangulate: get advice from several sources. Each person will have seen things from a different angle. That means they will see reality differently and will come up with different suggestions. Once you have a good idea of what the pattern of events really is, you can come up with the right course of action.

Political decision making

There is no such thing as a good idea which didn't happen. The first test of any idea or decision is whether it is implemented or not. This means you need to build a coalition of support for your decision. You try to do this by selling the brilliance of your idea. But do not be surprised when this results in everyone else shooting your idea down. If it is not their idea, then they have nothing to gain from supporting it, but much to gain from asking you awkward but 'helpful' questions. If you ignore their advice and things go wrong, you are in trouble. If you take their advice, then they can claim all the credit.

Instead of talking at people, listen to them. Ask what they would do. They may come up with good ideas. Even if they don't, the act of asking them gives them a sense of ownership and involvement in the process. The trick is to make sure you do not give them a veto over the entire decision. So make sure you ask finance about their advice on the financial aspects of the decision only; involve marketing in only the marketing aspects. You then retain control over the complete decision.

Once you have taken advice, you can return to each of your stakeholders and thank them for their brilliant insights and show how they have helped to shape the decision. Highlight the areas of agreement, so that they feel valued and involved: you want them to have ownership over the decision. If there is an area of real disagreement, ask them how they would resolve it. The best way to win is by cooperating, not fighting.

Emotional decision making

Making any decision involves risk. Rational risk is covered by risk assessments, risk logs and issue logs. These are relatively trivial risks. Because they are known and rational risks, it is relatively easy to find the required mitigating actions.

The greater risk is personal and emotional: if I make this decision, will I look like the office idiot? What will that do for my career?

This is why it is so hard to get people to support you and your idea. No one wants to join you as the office idiots. Saying 'no' is less risky than saying 'yes': people may get fired for costing the firm money as a result of a dumb idea. No one gets fired for stopping a good idea. You have to manage the emotional agenda, which is always unstated. You do this by de-risking the idea. This is another reason you do not ask experts to support the whole idea: you ask them to sign up on their particular area of expertise alone. Then, if it goes wrong they can distance themselves and there is no risk to them.

The larger the firm, the harder decision making becomes. Everyone wants to get involved, and anyone may veto your decision. Equally, there are few people brave enough to stick their heads above the parapet and make a decision. This is a wonderful opportunity. If you have the courage to make decisions, and the ability to sell the decision to the firm, you quickly acquire power and influence as someone who makes things happen. When others choose to hide, you can choose to shine.

The best way to win is by cooperating, not fighting.

02
Making decisions in uncertainty

Fortunately, decision making is hard and ambiguous. If it was easy, then we could all be replaced by a piece of software. Unfortunately, decision making is hard and ambiguous. It is also risky: no one wants to wear the dunce's cap for making the wrong decision.

Leaders have a few tried and trusted ways of making decisions in a world where we lack all the data we require, we lack the time and resources, and we face endless conflicting and changing pressures. The main principles for making decisions are:

- **Use your judgement.** If it is your decision, the chances are that you are the expert. Back your judgement.

- **Get advice.** But don't let your judgement be clouded by too many contradictory opinions. Often the main value of talking to other people is not to hear their point of view, but in making yourself articulate the pros and cons of each alternative. The more you talk, the more you will discover the sensible solution.

- **Follow the strategy and the values of the firm.** When a decision is very close, the chances are the strategy and values of the firm will drive you in one direction. For instance: should you give this customer a refund on this very marginal problem? That depends on whether your firm is profit-focused, process-focused or truly customer-focused. Many jobsworths will hide behind the process.

- **What would your boss do?** This may give you a clearer insight into the real priorities of your organization. Equally, if your team is looking for direction, let them decide. If it is their decision they will be committed to making it work; if it is your decision they may or may not be.

- **Focus on the outcome.** Don't fall into the trap of being obsessed with the immediate challenges and obstacles. Perhaps the next step is difficult, but if the outcome is big enough it is worth suffering the immediate pain for the later gain.

- **Build your coalition.** There is no such thing as a good idea which did not happen. A decision is only good if it is implemented. That means you need support. Decision making does not exist in a rational vacuum: it is also an intensely political exercise. Work out who the key stakeholders and influencers are; ask for their advice and slowly build a consensus for the decision you want.

> Decision making does not exist in a rational vacuum.
> It is also an intensely political exercise.

03
Effective meetings

There are three tests of an effective meeting. You can use them to decide if you want to attend a meeting or hold a meeting and who you want to attend. Each participant should be able to answer three questions at the end of the meeting:

1 What did I learn?

2 What did I contribute?

3 What do I do next?

If the participants have good answers for all three questions, it has been a good meeting for them. If they learnt nothing, contributed nothing and do nothing next, it was a failure for them and they should not have been there.

These tests help you avoid the just-in-case and face-time syndromes that convert a small meeting with the CEO into a major convention:

- **Just in case.** Executives bring all their bag carriers with them, because the bag carriers did the work and know the answers. They are there just in case an awkward question is asked. If executives do not know the answers, they are in the wrong meeting and possibly in the wrong job.

- **Face time.** Junior staff mistakenly believe that turning up at a meeting with the CEO and staying mute the whole time will impress the CEO. It does not. The CEO would rather staff were doing something useful with the organization's money.

Asking the three questions above sorts out those who *need* to be at the meeting from those who simply *want* to be at the meeting.

EXERCISE 6.1 Questions for meetings

Next time you arrange a meeting, think through the three questions for each person attending. If people will not have good answers at the end, do not invite them.

Next time you go to a meeting, go with your own agenda structured around the three points. It may be that your only action point is to catch a hard-to-get person informally at the meeting. Do not blindly accept the given agenda: make sure you know what you want to get out of the meeting and what you will contribute as well.

If executives do not know the answers, they are in the wrong meeting and possibly in the wrong job.

04
Managing projects

Principles

The outcomes of projects, like battles, are normally determined
before they start. The wise leader invests heavily in starting the
project right, before much time, money and effort are consumed
across the organization.

Projects normally fail because they succumb to one of the four
horsemen of the project apocalypse:

1 the wrong problem;

2 the wrong sponsor;

3 the wrong team;

4 the wrong process.

Figure 6.1 shows that the later you leave it, the harder it is to influence the final outcome. Heroic firefighting is futile near the end of
the project: by then the outcome is largely determined and the effort
has largely been spent. To ensure success, the leader must set the
project up for success from the very start.

> The outcomes of projects, like battles, are normally
> determined before they start.

Figure 6.1   Projects: effort and potential to influence the outcome

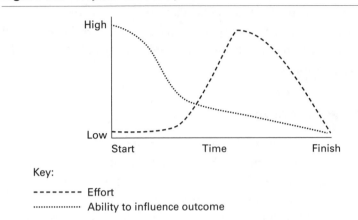

Key:

-------- Effort
·············· Ability to influence outcome

The four horsemen of the apocalypse

The wrong problem

The right problem is someone's red issue. Three tests of a red issue are:

1 The stakes for failure and success are high, and you can measure them in financial or non-financial terms.

2 The issue is not just important (solving climate change) but also urgent ('We will go bust next year if we don't...').

3 The organization is already working on the problem and is experiencing some setbacks. If no one is working on it, then is it really important and urgent?

The wrong sponsor

Someone must own the problem. That person will have the power and authority to implement the solution. A simple first test is to ask who needs to be involved in implementing the solution: the chances are that it will involve many people from across the organization. If the sponsor can bring these people together and get them to commit time, money and resource, he or she may be the right sponsor. A weak sponsor guarantees failure: he or she will not be able to remove the inevitable political roadblocks when the going gets tough.

The wrong team

Insist on the A-team. This is a fundamental test. If the project is important, the A-team will be put on it. The B-team is a sign that the project is not important and is a recipe for hell: it will never quite achieve the desired outcomes in the desired time to the desired quality, and it will keep on stumbling over hurdles that an A-team will leap over. The leader of a B-team will find that evenings, weekends and holidays disappear in a miasma of crises and chaos.

The wrong process

Most project planning gets hung up on this. If the first three horsemen of the apocalypse are avoided, this one vanishes as well. But no amount of good process will save a project if the first three horsemen are wreaking havoc.

> The leader of a B-team will find that evenings, weekends and holidays disappear in a miasma of crises and chaos.

Techniques

This is where geeks get very excited about Gantt and PERT charts and critical path analysis and come up with highly complex engineering-type diagrams that only they understand. Gantt and PERT charts are designed to help people who do not need help. The rest of humanity needs something simpler.

> Gantt and PERT charts are designed to help
> people who do not need help.

Here are some design principles for a good project plan:

- Do not start at the start. Start at the end with a very clear view of what needs to be achieved, summarized in 10 words maximum. If you start at the beginning, you will never get to the finish.

- Find the minimum number of steps required to get to the end: make it simple. This should show what critical steps happen in which order. Then create a timeline. Then drill down on each of the key steps to get as much detail as you wish.

- Find some early wins to create momentum. People want instant gratification and to believe they are backing a winner.

Here are some classic project planning traps:

- No clear deliverables, and conflicting expectations among stakeholders.

- No clear staging posts where progress can be reviewed and measured against goals.

- Excessive caution. If you need to do it, do it right and do it once. Investing just enough to lose is not smart. Running unrepresentative pilots and proofs of concept wastes time and achieves nothing.

- Process myopia. This is where the geeks fall in love with their process maps, risk logs, issues logs, meeting logs, telephone logs and master logs. The purpose of the project is to achieve an outcome, not run a perfect process.

- Poor governance structure and process (see below).

> If you start at the beginning, you will never get to the finish.

Governance

Senior managers can get very excited about starting a project, and then lose interest in the hard grind of seeing it through. Good governance of a project is essential to its success.

The best way to let a project spin out of control, fail to deliver and cost a fortune is as follows:

- Fail to put in formal governance procedures. Assume the consultants will do this for you.

- Make decisions, when they are needed, slowly. Indecision kills projects and kills morale.

- Change your mind quite often.

Good governance is not rocket science. Have a clear governance structure. Create a RACI chart for the programme:

- **R = responsibilities.** Who is responsible for delivering which part of the programme? There should be clear lines of accountability: it should be clear who gets praised or kicked at the end of the project, and for what.

- **A = authority.** Who has ultimate authority for making decisions, approving budgets and reviewing progress? There should be only one authorizer per project. The authorizer also has ultimate accountability for the project. The authorizer is powerful and may not be involved day to day, but will call the project into existence and conclude it; in between, the authorizer may help remove political roadblocks and monitor progress.

- **C = cooperation.** Whose cooperation is required and who needs to be consulted for what (eg finance may need to check your figures, but are not responsible for delivering the project)?

- **I = involvement.** Who else needs to be involved (by providing expertise, assistance, etc) or needs to be kept informed?

Have a clear governance process in addition to the structure. The basics are easy and normally ignored:

- regular updates and review sessions;
- standardized reports;
- rapid and effective decision-making processes.

Indecision kills projects and kills morale.

05
Setting goals

Goal setting in a car factory is easy. The work is standardized; you have objective measures of quality and throughput and you can see if people are working or not. None of this applies to office work. Goal setting in an office is hard for three reasons:

1 **Ambiguous work.** The nature of managerial work is ambiguous. It is often unclear when a task is complete, and assessing quality is even harder. If you have to produce a report, there is always more you can find out and more you can add. It is never complete, even after the deadline. This is one of the reasons managerial work is tough: if you are diligent, then you will always feel that there is more you can do and should do.

2 **Variable work.** You are not producing so many cars a day; you need your team to chase decisions, fix suppliers, prepare reports, work with other departments. This makes it impossible to assess productivity. You are always attempting to compare apples and bicycles. It is a pointless exercise.

3 **Variable capabilities.** Your team will have different levels of capability, which will not be apparent from the outset. Some team members will be good at some things, less good at others. And teams change over time: experienced team members move on and new team members start who will be an unknown quantity.

The standard approach to setting goals is to set SMART goals. SMART is an acronym with many variations. Here is what it typically stands for:

- **Specific**: know what it is you want to achieve.

- **Measurable**: measures can be financial, non-financial, quantitative or qualitative. You only get what you measure, so make sure you have good measures.

- **Actionable or assignable**: know who is going to be responsible for making it happen.

- **Relevant or realistic**: ensure it meets a business need and can be achieved.

- **Time bound**: be clear about when it must be finished and when you will check progress.

Clearly, this is better than the opposite sort of goals: vague, unmeasurable, unactionable, irrelevant, impossible and with no deadline. But in a world of ambiguous and variable work, SMART goals can be hard to achieve. But get as close as you can. In a world of ambiguity and uncertainty, your team craves clarity. The more clarity you can create for your team, the better.

There is one missing element from SMART. How ambitious should your goals be, for yourself and your team? If you believe that SMART goals should be realistic, the chances are that you will always underachieve. Realism is code for caution. You do not change the world, or the firm, by being deeply cautious. As a leader, your role is to take people where they would not have got by themselves. That means you should be ambitious. The 'S' in SMART should stand for 'Stretching' not 'Specific'.

An ambitious goal is one which is noticed, and relevant, at least two levels above you in the firm. If you are at the top of the firm, an ambitious goal is one which causes your team to suck breath over their gums as they realize the scale of your ambition. Here is why it pays to be ambitious in goal setting:

- It is easier to gain support for a big idea than a small idea: big ideas engage powerful people, and once you have them on your side, then you can attract the team and resources to make it happen. Once you succeed, you will be marked out as a future leader.

- As a leader your job is to make a difference, not to manage the status quo. Your firm needs people who step up and take the firm forwards.

- Your team will only learn and grow by taking on big challenges. They learn nothing from doing more of the same. The more they learn and grow and achieve ambitious goals, the more they will want to work for you. You will become the leader people want to follow.

- You will personally learn and grow from being ambitious, and you will be noticed and supported more by both bosses and team members.

- Management lives in the legacy of scientific management, which is meant to be rational and reasonable. As a leader, you need to do better than that. Learn the art of unreasonable leadership. Be unreasonable and inflexible in setting highly ambitious goals, but be reasonable, supportive and flexible in how your team reaches the goal.

In a world of ambiguity and uncertainty, your team craves clarity.

06
Selling and persuading

Features, benefits and dreams

Selling is not just for salespeople. All leaders constantly have to sell themselves, their ideas and new initiatives. If you cannot sell, you cannot lead.

First, do not think only about what you are selling. You may be very excited about your idea. The bigger question is why your listener should be interested in your idea. Your enthusiasm for a new way of cleaning toilets may fire you up, but not everyone is necessarily excited about toilet cleaning. So you have to get into their shoes and into their heads and see the world through their eyes. You have to start not with your idea, but with their problem.

Everyone is selling: ideas, proposals and social events. We normally sell at three levels:

1 features ('My computer has 8GB RAM memory');

2 benefits ('It can handle video editing');

3 dreams ('It could turn me into a Hollywood mogul').

Features are about the product and rarely appeal to anyone except geeks. Features are things like engine size and the alphabet soup of technical specs for your computer. Benefits are unique to each person and are more compelling. These are things like 'Daz washes whiter' and 'This car goes faster/is safer.' But if you can tap into people's dreams then you are winning. These are things like:

- You will look cool and successful in this car/jacket, etc.
- Presentation training will help you with your amateur dramatics skills and ambitions.
- This diet/facelift/Botox makes you look young and sexy.

Avoid selling features. At least work out the benefits, or ideally the dreams, that will appeal to the person you are selling to. Start with what the person wants, not with what you have.

EXERCISE 6.2   Selling features, benefits and dreams

Work out how to sell the following, using features, benefits and dreams. Then see which sounds most convincing:

- a fridge to a desert nomad, a local family and an Inuit;
- an off-road car to a school mum, a farmer and a football star;
- a pencil to an illiterate tribesman, a child and a cosmonaut.

If you can tap into people's dreams then you are winning.

Tapping into people's minds

We have already met fear, greed, idleness and risk in motivation skills. We meet them again in selling skills. They work together:

- **Fear:** What problem am I solving for the other person?
- **Greed:** What hope or dream am I helping the other person achieve?

- **Idleness and risk**: Am I making it easy for the other person to agree? Have I removed the risks he or she perceives?

Do not start with your product, idea or perspective. The other person does not care about it. The starting point is that person's hopes, fears, dreams and risks. You can use this not just for selling soap powder. You can use it for selling your project, your idea or your proposal to peers and bosses alike: tap into their natural fear, greed, idleness and risk aversion.

As a simple exercise, look at how you might use hopes, fears, idleness and risk to sell an off-road vehicle to a school-run parent and to a business person (see Table 6.1). Now do the same exercise with selling a mobile phone. In both cases you will probably find:

- Trying to focus on features such as engine size is not very compelling.

- The selling proposition varies dramatically depending on who you are selling to. You succeed when you focus less on the product and more on the buyer's needs.

Table 6.1 Using hopes, fears, idleness and risk in selling

	Off-road vehicle (school-run parent)	Off-road vehicle (business person)
Hopes: What the person wants.	Show you are a caring parent: and be one up on other parents.	Look cool, affluent and adventurous: and look down on lesser mortals.
Fears: What is the fear this might remove?	Safety for children.	Very safe in bad weather.
Idleness: How do I make it easy for the person to buy and use?	We will fit child locks and seats for you.	No hassle: insurance and servicing included.
Risk: How do I eliminate the perceived risk of purchase/use?	Your spouse will like it as well.	Other business people buy this (you will not look stupid in this car).

● The way you convey the message is not the same as the message. The salesperson will not say 'This car is for snobs' but will hint at the status associated with the car ('This is a limited-edition version; many people want it, but few can afford it'; 'It seems to be very popular with rock stars/explorers/people with country estates', etc).

> Do not start with your product, idea or perspective.

The selling process

It is not enough to know what to sell. You also need to know how to sell. Here is a classic seven-step sales cycle:

1 Agree the problem/opportunity.

2 Preview the benefits of addressing the problem/opportunity.

3 Suggest the idea.

4 Explain how it works.

5 Pre-empt objections.

6 Reinforce the benefits.

7 Close.

Check reactions at each stage. The cycle can take from 30 seconds (suggesting a dinner date) to years (selling a fleet of aircraft). The most important step is the first: agree the problem/opportunity from the buyer's perspective. Until you know what the buyer wants/needs, you do not know what you are selling.

Consider the example of suggesting a drink after a long day at work using the seven-step cycle:

1 'It's been a hard day.'

2 'We all need to relax.'

3 'Let's go for a quick drink.'

4 'The pub is next door.'

5 'I'll buy the first round.'

6 'We can all unwind there.'

7 'Last person out, turn off the lights.'

When you start, this process can feel complicated. Get used to it and it soon becomes second nature. Ideally, the process is a conversation in which you let the other person talk. You simply use the process to check where you are in the conversation and where you want to guide it next.

There are two important exceptions to following this process. First, if the person is ready to agree with you, move straight to the close. At this stage, the more you say, the more you are giving the person the opportunity to rethink the decision and say no. Many sales have been lost by the seller getting overenthusiastic and carrying the conversation on for too long. Second, if you find the other person starting to make objections, you have three choices:

1 Respond to each objection. This is obvious, but highly dangerous. You may well find that, instead of helping the conversation, you land up in an increasingly bitter argument. The reason for this is that you may well not have understood the problem that you are solving for the other person, so the best course of action is often option 2.

2 Quietly go back to the start and make sure you understand the problem. This avoids an argument and gets you both back to agreeing with each other.

3 Finally, you may decide that the objections are not substantive: they may well be an emotional and automatic response. Do not respond rationally to such objections: it simply invites an argument. Great salespeople find ways of ducking the objection completely by changing the subject, distracting the person or making a joke. The buyer rarely wants to repeat a half-baked objection, so will be happy to move on with you.

EXERCISE 6.3   The sales process

Go back to the fridge, the car and the pencil in Exercise 6.2. Try selling them using the seven-step framework.

Until you know what the buyer wants/needs to buy, you do not know what you are selling.

The art of the close

Buyers are not mind-readers. They do not know what you want them to do. You have to ask them: you have to close the discussion and the sale. This causes some salespeople to panic. In reality, it is easy. The buyer is expecting you to ask for something, otherwise that person would be wasting his or her time talking to you. So make sure you ask and close.

When someone is ready to agree, let the person agree by closing the sale. Bank it. Do not go on selling: you may land up unselling by mistake.

There are four main ways of closing a sale/discussion:

1 **The alternative close**: 'Do you want the red car or would you prefer the blue one?' You are not offering the choice of no car. Sneaky and effective.

2 **The action close**: 'Here are the car keys. Just sign on the line and I will guide your new car out of the showroom.'

3 **The direct close**: 'Do you want to buy the car?' Very dangerous: the person might say 'No'.

4 **The assumed close**: 'So we are all agreed that we are buying a fleet of pink and yellow cars.' Often used by those chairing meetings.

The classic mistake for managers is to leave a meeting without clear next steps: you make your pitch, you deal with objections, you carry the day and everyone is happy. But as you leave the room, you realize that no next steps have been agreed: triumph has been turned into disaster. You always have to leave with clear next steps, even if the next step is only that you will meet again at an agreed time.

In practice, this means you always need a Plan A and a Plan B before every meeting. Plan A is what you intend to achieve, and you have to make sure you close the meeting to do so. But the unexpected can happen and Plan A can become impossible. Some people are quick on their feet and can work out their escape route, their Plan B, in real time. For the rest of us, preparation is key. We need a clear Plan B so that if Plan A unravels, we do not panic: we still have a viable way to close the meeting with clear next steps.

EXERCISE 6.4 Closing

Try all four types of close for the car and the mobile phone from earlier in this chapter.

Note down each time you are in a meeting how effectively people close and what lines they use. Start building your own list of effective closes. If a close fails, look back and see what went wrong:

- Check against fear, greed, idleness and risk.
- Check against features, hopes and dreams.
- Check against the seven-step sales process.
- Check against the close.

Buyers are not mind-readers. They are expecting you to ask for something.

The ultimate secret

Great leaders and great salespeople share a common secret: they have two ears and one mouth.

> **EXERCISE 6.5**   Have you got what it takes?
>
> Count the number of ears and mouths you have. You may well share the secret of great leaders and salespeople.

The ultimate secret is that great leaders and salespeople not only have two ears and one mouth: they use them in that proportion. They listen at least twice as much as they talk. You will be surprised at how often managers talk themselves into submission, buyers talk themselves into buying and lovers talk themselves into bed. Let people listen to their favourite voice, their own, and they will think that you are wonderful.

Listening skills are covered in Part Five, Section 5. Once you can really listen, understand and learn, you are on the path to success. You may think that listening is just a sneaky sales trick – it is. But it is also much more than that. When you are in a meeting with senior people, observe closely who does the most talking: it is normally the more junior people, who are pitching their ideas to the more senior people. The senior people, like judges in a courtroom, have all the power and need to ask a little and say even less. Talking less and listening more is the privilege of power.

> Let people listen to their favourite voice: their own.

> **EXERCISE 6.6**   Listening
>
> Try it. Here are a few hints to help you reflect on an important discussion:
>
> ● Who was asking more questions? If you were focused on answers not questions, you were probably talking more than listening.

- Write down how much you learnt from the other person: if you have fully understood the other person's hopes, fears and dreams you were probably listening well.

- Ask a neutral third party who they thought was doing the talking versus the listening.

Leaders and salespeople not only have two ears and one mouth;
they use them in that proportion.

07
Managing change

Are you ready to change?

Change is about people. Most sane people do not like change. Change involves hard work and risk:

- Will I still have a job after the change?
- Who will my boss be?
- Will I need new skills?
- Will I succeed?

When you hear people object to change, you will hear very rational arguments against change. Listen behind the rational arguments and you will hear emotional fears and political objections to what you propose. Worst of all, you will hear the overwhelming silence of apathy: doing precisely nothing is the best way to defeat change.

The first test is to know if your organization is ready to change. Use the change equation to figure this out. Here it is in all its spurious mathematical accuracy. Change succeeds when:

$$N \times V \times C \times F > R$$

EXERCISE 6.7   Is your organization ready for change?

Use the change equation to see how ready your team is for change:

- **N = need for change**. How much pain and threat do people experience with the way things are at the moment?

- **V = vision of the end result**. Does the team see the benefits of change?

- **C = capability and credibility**. Does the team have the capability to change, and do you have a successful track record of change?

- **F = first steps**. Are there some practical first steps that build momentum, achieve some early wins and build confidence?

- **R = risks and costs of change**. How large are the personal, political and financial costs of the change?

Repeat this exercise for each individual to see how ready he or she is to change, and repeat it for the organization as a whole.

Most sane people do not like change.

The cycle of change

Change rarely runs smoothly. The initial burst of enthusiasm gets submerged in the trench warfare of detail, opposition and setbacks. You cannot eliminate these challenges. But you can at least set expectations so that no one is surprised by what happens.

The change cycle normally follows the pattern shown in Figure 6.2:

- **Stage 1**: The enthusiasm of an early start with some early wins.

- **Stage 2**: The fall into despair as the challenges and the opposition mount.

- **Stage 3**: The valley of death. This is where it seems that things cannot get worse. This stage can be good news: the opposition shows that people are engaging in the change and discovering its scale and importance. At this stage, the true leaders emerge: future-focused, solution-focused and action-focused, while everyone else is wallowing in a slough of despond.

Figure 6.2   Change and the valley of death

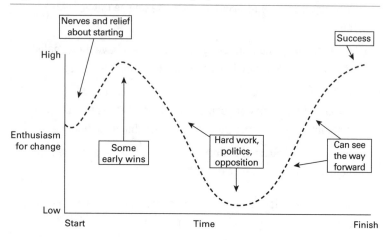

- **Stage 4:** The roller coaster moves back up as everyone else starts to see that success is possible. Enthusiasm builds the closer everyone gets to the finish line.

EXERCISE 6.8   Leading through the valley of death

In the valley of death, the leader focuses on solutions and actions, while everyone else is indulging in an orgy of doubt:

- **Step 1**: Write down on a piece of paper all the rational, political and emotional objections to your next change programme.
- **Step 2**: Throw away the piece of paper.
- **Step 3**: What are you going to do to make the change happen, solve the problems and bring the objectors on board (or isolate them)?

Remember, people reach levels of readiness for change at different times. Helping people adjust to change takes time.

The leader focuses on solutions and actions, while everyone else is indulging in an orgy of doubt.

08
Reorganizing

Rationale

Some people naively believe that reorganizations are about finding the perfect organization structure. Over the years, such naivety turns to cynicism as they see the corporate carousel turn full circle time and again: centralize and decentralize and back again; functional to product to geographic to customer focus and back again; another delayering, which only seems to add more layers and confusion.

In practice, a leader can use a reorganization to achieve three outcomes:

1 **Improve the organization structure.** This is in line with received wisdom. Changing conditions require changing responses, so no single organization structure will remain perfect for long.

2 **Change the balance of power.** Some leaders are like weak monarchs who are held to ransom by powerful barons. Moving the power barons around, with perhaps a ritual execution of one or two, has a powerful effect on the barons: they start to respect the power of the monarch and, cut off from their old fiefdoms, become more dependent on the patronage of the monarch. Every leader needs to put in place their preferred team: a reorganization is therefore as much about people and politics as it is about structure and logic.

3 **Reset expectations.** A reorganization is a perfect opportunity to change the psychological contract between the leader and individual team members. This is not just about performance goals: it is a two-way conversation about styles, how they should work together and what needs to change in future.

In theory, a leader reorganizes with the aim of designing the right organization structure to support the corporate strategy. This is the rational method advocated by consultants. Back in the real world, most leaders intuitively reorganize the right way; they start by looking at the people they have, and then they work out how to deploy them to best effect. The result may be theoretically suboptimal, but it is practically the best thing to do.

> Moving the power barons around, with perhaps a ritual execution of one or two, has a powerful effect.

The need for speed

Reorganize fast. Reorganize once. Remove the uncertainty as fast as you can, and then focus on building the business.

The best time to reorganize is when you start in a new position. Most CEOs alter their top team when they are appointed. There are three reasons for this:

1 They put the right leadership team in place as soon as possible: a dysfunctional leadership team is not good for the organization.

2 They minimize the FUD factor: fear, uncertainty and doubt. The longer you leave it, the more the FUD factor rises, politicking increases and morale collapses.

3 They avoid getting trapped in the old ways and the old psychological contract. It makes change, not stability, the way of life.

Speed is particularly important when 'letting people go'. If you have to kill someone, at least be humane and do it quickly. The legal fetish for due process simply spins the agony out for everyone: the victim hangs on desperately for the last breath of corporate air; the executioner boss feels in turn embarrassed, frustrated, angry and sympathetic; and the organization is transfixed by the trauma being played out. Move the person out as fast as you can. Then concentrate your efforts on the survivors: they are your future. They need to be assured that you are not continuing to swing your axe randomly: they need to focus on doing a good job, rather than jockeying for survival.

If you have to kill someone, at least be humane and do it quickly.

09
Selecting your team

Building your team

How many effective working hours are you capable of delivering every day, every year? Allow for all the distractions of social media, time-wasting meetings and pointless bureaucracy. Three hours, four hours a day? More?

The answer is that you can deliver countless thousands of hours of great work every day, if you have the right team to deliver it for you. As a leader, your job is not to make things happen yourself. Your job is to make things happen through other people. So how do you build the right sort of team, and what does a good team look like?

The right sort of team has two qualities: balance and values.

Balance

An orchestra of the 50 best conductors in the world might be talented, but it would not be much good. The trap for all leaders is to hire people like yourself. This has the virtue of making life easy, because everyone thinks the same way. But if you are the equivalent of the orchestra's conductor, you will land up with an orchestra of conductors. Balance has to balance skills and styles:

- **Balance of skills.** Most team leaders understand this. You need people with different skills to fill different roles. If you hate bookkeeping, then learn to love bookkeepers. Let the rest of the team do what you are unwilling or unable to do.

- **Balance of styles.** Many leaders struggle with this. They want to hire people like themselves, because they are easy to understand. But a good team needs different perspectives and different approaches. You need people who can see the big picture, and others who can sweat the detail; you need the great analysts and the great people managers; you need people who are good with words and good with numbers; you need thoughtful and expressive people. There may be the odd superhero out there who is all of these things. But the easier way forward is to make sure that you have balanced the strengths and styles of each team member. Diversity is more than race, sex and religion: it is about how people think and interact.

Values

You can train skills, but you cannot train values. And not all values are good. So it makes sense to hire to values, not just to skills. Ideally, you will find both the right skills and right values in the same person. But if you have to compromise, compromise on the skills: the person with the right values will learn and grow fast.

Values do not mean the garbage which firms produce in values statements or put on brass plaques. Values are about what you want to see from your team day to day. Make your own list of what you want and what you do not want; for instance:

- Hard work, honesty, diligence, being fast to learn and adapt, being positive, treating people with respect.

- Evades responsibility, settles for 'good enough', fixed way of thinking, does not learn or adapt, cynical, abrasive with peers.

We have all seen team members who have plenty of the first set of values, and they are a joy to work with. We can all remember enduring individuals with too many of the second set of values: we know that they will not change their ways.

Once you know the values you want on your team, look in the mirror. How well do you embody those values? The values of your team will reflect your values. Use your target values to hold yourself to account. Behave as you want others to behave.

Many leaders come to the realization that they hire for skills and fire for (the wrong) values. Do not make that mistake. Hire to values, not just to skills.

10
Developing your team

Growing your team

Leadership is a two-way street. As a leader, you should expect your team to perform for you. Equally, your team has expectations of you. In the short term, you need to manage their workloads and set them up for success. In the longer term, you have to look after their career interests. This is more than going into battle for them once a year to secure them the right bonus and promotions. It is about helping them all grow and develop so that they can succeed in the long term. You have to help them on the journey that you are also taking.

You have three ways of helping your team thrive. Use all three.

Training

Training is the focus of most development, and it is often the least useful approach. Team members are normally happy to go on training for technical subjects such as understanding accounting or using spreadsheets. There is a clear transfer of knowledge and a clear payback from attending. But you can be the world's best expert at spreadsheets and be the world's worst leader.

When you ask your team to go on training for leadership or soft skills, you will hear a litany of excuses for why they cannot go. There are two reasons why people try to avoid such courses:

1 **Perception of weakness:** Going on a training programme about managing people is seen as an insult. It implies that you are no good at managing people and you are having to remediate a weakness.

2 **Variable quality:** some courses are great, others are rubbish. Once you have spent a day being told to guess what the facilitator with their franchised theory wants to write on a flip chart, you never want to go again, even if the drinks at the end of the day are free.

The reality is that even with the best training course, you cannot arrive at 9 am knowing little about leadership and emerge at 5 pm as a great leader. Training may help at the margins, but you need other tools to support your team.

Coaching

You are your team's #1 trainer. And the best way to train people is not to tell them what to do, but to let them discover what works best for them. That is the essence of coaching, which is covered in detail elsewhere in the book.

You may be the #1 trainer, but you are not the only coaching resource for your team. You can unleash two other coaching resources for your team.

First, get your team members to help and coach each other. At its simplest, this is about creating a problem-solving culture. The more the team helps each other, the less they rely on you. Your workload goes down and you can focus on wherever you think you will add the most value.

Second, get each team member to coach themselves. You are your own best coach. Help each team member learn the basic questions of coaching; help them learn the structure of the coaching conversation. Slowly, they will internalize the dialogue. They will not need to turn to you or other team members for help. They will develop themselves.

Experience

Experience is only valuable if we learn from it. That is why it is vital for team members to learn to coach themselves.

As the team leader, you have to help your team have the right experiences to help them grow and develop. Clearly, this is not possible all the time. There will always be dull and routine work which does not stretch or develop people. It may be boring, but it is necessary. As the team leader you need to balance routine work with work which challenges and stretches each team member.

If you succeed, you will end up promoting and losing your best team members, which is a perverse incentive for you. But in reality, this means you will be leading a team that the best and the brightest want to join: you will be seen as the high road to success.

Helping others succeed is a great way to help yourself succeed.

Experience is only valuable if you learn from it.

Part Seven
Political skills

01
Influencing people

Leadership used to be relatively simple: you led people you controlled. Now leadership is harder. You have to lead people you do not control. If you want to make things happen, you have to work with other departments, with other firms, with your customers and suppliers to succeed. You cannot control the people you need, but you can influence them. Influence lets you stretch your power far beyond your formal authority limits.

Influence is the key skill for leaders of the future to learn. Here are 10 ways you can influence people positively. You do not have to be expert at all of them. Try one or two techniques to start with. Even these will make a difference. As you master one technique, add another. Slowly you will find yourself acquiring the magic of influence. No one else will quite be sure how you do it. This is your magic sauce:

1 **Build rapport.** People trust people like themselves, so find out what you have in common professionally, personally and in terms of experience.

2 **Align your agendas.** Find out how they see the world, what they need, want and fear. Work your agenda to fit with theirs: don't start with your agenda and mindlessly inflict it on them. When you see the world through their eyes, you can start to influence them better.

3 **Listen.** The more you listen, the more you find out about them and the more they relax. Let people talk about their favourite subject: themselves. Look interested. Smart questions work better than smart ideas.

4 **Flatter.** There is no point at which flattery becomes counterproductive: no one thinks they are over-promoted, over-recognized and overpaid. If you recognize their innate genius, diligence and humanity they will be in awe of your very fine judgement and they will reciprocate.

5 **Build commitment incrementally.** Don't ask for everything all at once: don't scare them. Ask for small commitments and limited involvement. Let the commitments build.

6 **Build your trust and credibility.** Always deliver on your commitments. Credibility is like a vase: hard to build and easy to break. Once broken, it is hard to repair and is never really the same again. So be crystal clear about what you commit to: it is better to have a difficult conversation before committing to action than to be making excuses after the event.

7 **Manage risk.** People are risk averse. Remove perceived risk and personal risk. Perceptions may be false, but the consequences of perceptions are real. Understand how others see the world and see risk and manage that reality. Your world view is not the universal world view. Their world view is the reality they live with, so understand it and manage it.

8 **Put scarcity to work.** Find something they want which you can give. And then make them work for it: they will value it more than if you give it away.

9 **Something for something.** Reciprocity works. Don't give something for nothing: it sets the wrong expectations. This is the tit-for-tat principle: ensure that they see there are positive and negative consequences to their actions.

10 **Act the part: the partnership principle.** Act as their partner and equal, not as a supplicant. You want an adult-to-adult conversation, not a parent–child conversation. You will be treated as you appear.

Let people talk about their favorite subject: themselves.

02
Achieving influence and power

It is hard to influence a person. It is even harder to influence a firm. But if you want to make things happen, you have to have influence across the firm as a whole. Part of that comes from having the right networks of influence: you have to know the right people and they have to want to work with you. But influence and power are more than simply knowing the right people.

Having looked at 10 strategies for influencing individuals, here are six strategies for becoming influential across the firm:

1 **Be ambitious, for yourself and your firm.** The world remembers Alexander the Great who conquered the known world by the age of 30: that was an insane task for the king of a tinpot state on the edge of civilization. Who remembers his cousin Alexander the Reasonable? Leaders lead people where they would not have got by themselves. Your ambitious agenda will help your firm, your team and yourself.

2 **Take control.** Many people in leadership positions are not leading. They are in role, but not in power. They are simply administering a legacy they have inherited. To take control, you need three things:

   – *Idea.* Your idea will show how you will make a difference. Big ideas beat small ideas every time.

   – *People.* You have to build the right team. Do not assume that the team you inherited is the team you need for the future.

   – *Money.* You can't change the world without balancing the books. Money is the rocket fuel of ambition, so fight for the right budget. But beware. A big budget without a big idea is a waste of time and effort. The idea always comes first. If your idea and your team are genuinely good, then the money will follow. If the money is not there, then either people do not believe in your idea or they do not believe in your team, including you.

3 **Build your network of support.** Your network will consist of decision makers, decision influencers, and all the key functions which can support you or sabotage you. Staff departments may not be able to approve your plans, but they can stop your plans. It is easy to think of them as a burden; treat them with respect and they will treat you with respect.

4 **Align your agenda with top management.** Make sure that what you are doing is relevant and useful to top management. Those boring speeches, e-mails and conferences have a purpose: they signal what top management want to achieve. If you show you understand what they want and you are proactive in finding ways of helping them achieve their goals, you will suddenly find yourself with friends in high places.

5 **Seize the moment.** At moments of truth leaders step up, others step back. There are four sorts of moment when you can see power shifting from one person to another. They are the moments you become a leader, even if you do not have the title:

- *Crises.* There are always crises in firms when many people want to duck or to point the finger of blame. Be the person who looks forward to what can be done, rather than looks back to what has been done. Focus on the solution, not the problem. Become the 'man – or woman – with the plan'.

- *Conflict.* Firms are set up for conflict. It is through constructive conflict that the priorities of the firm are decided and the resources of the firm are allocated. Do not duck conflict, but engage with it positively, so that you can protect and promote your agenda and your needs.

- *Ambiguity.* There will be times when no one is quite sure what to do or who should do it. Many people will hide behind analysis and having meetings: this gives the impression of action without the risk of doing anything. The brave move to action, not analysis. By moving to action, you take control and you become the leader.

- *New initiatives.* Initiatives are always starting, either in response to external challenges, or to top management ideas. There is never the management capacity to deal with these new ideas, especially when they are first being thought about. Strike as early as possible: help shape the idea. You can then lead it, knowing that it is shaped the way you want.

6 **Pick your battles.** Most corporate battles are pointless. But you do need to know when to stand up and protect your interests. But if you are going to fight, follow the three rules of corporate warfare, which were originally laid down by Chinese philosopher Sun Tzu over 2,000 years ago:

- Only fight when there is a prize worth fighting for;

- Only fight when you know you will win;

- Only fight when there is no other way of achieving your goal.

Normally, it is better to win a friend than it is to win an argument. The times you have to stand up are around budgets, assignments, resourcing and team selection. Get these right and life is manageable; get them wrong and you invite a year of stress and underachievement.

> At moments of truth, leaders step up; others step back.

03
Influencing decisions

The art of management is about making things happen through people you do not control. This means you have to use influence as much as power. And influence is essential when it comes to all the critical decisions that affect you and your role: budgets, staffing, assignments, priorities, etc.

The classic work on influencing decisions was written by the Nobel Prize winner Daniel Hahnemann. Let's save you the trouble of reading all his works, and focus on the main lessons we can draw from his research:

- **Anchoring.** Is the diameter of the moon more or less than 8,000 km? I have no idea. But I have just anchored the debate on 8,000 km. The way to anchor a debate is to follow the motto of the Welsh rugby team in the 1980s: 'Get your retaliation in first.' Set the terms of the debate early, and on the question you want answered. Do you want next year's budget debate to be anchored on achieving a 15 per cent cost reduction or on a 5 per cent increase (with an increase in revenues)? If you let the planning department set the terms of the debate, you will probably be answering the wrong question.

- **Social proof.** If we wear the same gear as our sports heroes, perhaps we can play like them. Some hope. But the power of endorsement is great: if it is good enough for the champions, it should be good enough for us. You do not need to get an Olympic champion to support your latest idea; you need to find powerful sponsors inside your organization who will endorse your idea. Senior managers are like venture capitalists: they do not judge the quality of the idea alone; they judge the quality of the people backing the idea. Find good sponsors.

- **Repetition.** All advertisers and dictators have discovered the same eternal truth: repetition works. Repetition works. Repetition works. Repetition works. Repetition works. Repetition works. Repetition works. Repetition works. What works? Repetition works! Never tire of hammering the same message home time and time again. Eventually people start to remember it and even to believe it.

- **Emotional relevance.** Most human beings find their eyes glazing over when presented with endless data and analysis. And we have all got so used to lobbyists, politicians and even sponsored scientists making dodgy claims based on dodgy and partial use of statistics that few of us believe any more. But we believe what we see. So if the latest employment figures show unemployment is up by 15,000, who cares? I have a job and all is well. If the company starts cutting back, then clearly the economy is in a bit of a mess. If my job is cut then we are not just in recession, but a major depression. If you want to make your case, make it vivid. Use a killer factoid. For instance: 'We say we have a performance culture, but in the last 20 years more people have died in service than been fired for poor performance.' Or make it emotionally intense. Instead of showing research about customer dissatisfaction, show a video clip, recording or social media feed of a customer going nuts as a result of poor service.

- **Restricted choice.** Give people 37 options to choose from and they will be paralysed by indecision: they will inevitably fear that they have not chosen the best option. Make it simple. Give them a choice of at most three: the cheap and nasty option, the brilliant but absurdly expensive option and the option you want them to pick.

- **Loss aversion and risk.** No one wants to be the fool who made a bad decision. And risk is not just about rational risk. Real risk is personal and emotional: 'How will I be seen if I make this decision?' So help people look good. Give them a story they can tell their colleagues about why they made a smart decision. Think about buying a car: we all have tales to tell about how we got a good deal. We got a great trade-in price, cheap financing, some free extras, free servicing or extended warranty. Be assured, however: the dealer was not losing money. You have a great story, and the dealer has made a tidy profit.

- **Smart managers work the flip side of risk.** They show that the risk of doing nothing greatly exceeds the risk of doing something. 'If we do not spend £100 million on renewing our systems, then the current systems will fall over and we will be out of business.' Use risk to your advantage.

- **Incremental commitment.** Retail companies use this trick endlessly. 'Three months' free trial period...' and by then you are hooked or it is just too much effort to switch. Internet companies do this: you spend 10 minutes working through the website to arrange your flight, and then you get hit with the booking charge, the delivery charge, the credit card charge: again, it is just too much effort to start again and look for another provider. You can use the same trick. Don't ask for the £2 million commitment right away. Ask to do an initial scoping phase, or a pilot, or a test market: build momentum. Once momentum is built, people find it harder to stop it than to let it continue.

- **A radical alternative: just do it.** Sometimes, it is easier to ask forgiveness than it is to ask for permission. So assume that you have approval and move ahead. This puts the onus on others to stop you. They may not want to give you permission, but they also do not want to pick a fight: it is too much effort and too risky. So they let you proceed. But make sure you succeed; there will be plenty of people who will be very happy to kick you when you are down.

> The risk of doing nothing greatly exceeds
> the risk of doing something.

04
Learning to say 'no'

This is a critical skill for any leader. Saying 'no' to a boss can be a career limiting move. But agreeing to nonsense is also a recipe for stress and disaster. The art is to say no without appearing negative.

In practice, saying no is tough because very often you are ambushed by an idea and you are put in a position where you feel the need to respond yes or no. The first principle comes from the need to avoid the 'commitment ambush' by buying time.

The art of buying time

When you are asked to take something on, go along with a new idea or support some initiative, you need time to think. You can buy time by asking questions. At all costs, avoid giving answers. The temptation may be to curry favour by going along with an idea for a while. You will then find yourself quickly committed to a course of action that you will slowly regret.

Use the principles of coaching (Part Three, Section 6) to work out how to ask questions that will sound constructive. The goal is to ask open questions and follow the coaching model:

- **Agree the goal of the idea:**
  - What is the problem this idea solves? For whom?
  - What are the benefits of doing this? For whom?

- Understand the context:
  - Who is sponsoring this?
  - What are the time frames?
  - What support and resources will be available?
  - Why are we looking at this now?
  - How does this fit with our other priorities?
- Create and evaluate options:
  - How else can this be achieved?
- Identify the obstacles to success.
- Conclude.

By the time you have gone through the first four sets of questions, time will have elapsed to let you think and you will have gathered enough information to make an informed decision about what you want to do. You may even want to say yes instead of no. It is also possible that the other person will have talked him or herself out of the original idea and into another, better idea.

As a leader you will be coming up with ideas you want others to agree to. Now turn the model on its head: work out what all your answers to the questions above will be. You may convince yourself you need a better idea: at least you will have saved yourself the embarrassment of suggesting a half-baked one. But if you can answer all the questions clearly, then you probably have a good idea and are well placed for a discussion with others about it.

> At all costs, avoid giving answers.

The cheese shop game: 'no' with no 'no'

Leaders know 'no' is a no-no in corporate life. Saying no makes you look negative and not action-focused. But occasionally you need to stop insanity happening. You have been through the coaching method of reviewing an idea, but it's still floating around like a bee with a bad attitude and a big sting. You need to do something to get rid of it. Welcome to the cheese shop game.

The cheese shop game

The cheese shop game was devised by Monty Python. A shopper enters the cheese shop and asks for a named cheese like Stilton or Cheddar. The shop owner has to find a way of saying that he has not got that cheese without saying he has not got it. Excuses might be things like:

'Sorry, out of season...'.

'Haven't you heard about the health scare?'

'Right out of fashion.'

'I wouldn't sell that to my dog.'

The person who first runs out of cheeses to name or excuses to offer, loses.

The corporate cheese shop game

In the corporate version of the cheese shop game, you have to find reasons for resisting an idea without saying no to the idea. There are three main routes of defence for you:

1 Priorities:

   – 'How does this fit with my other priorities? Which ones would you like me to defer for this idea?'

   – 'Should we do this before or after X episode (which is more urgent/on the critical path)?'

2 Process:

   – 'Could we do it this other way instead?' (better, faster, cheaper, less risky).

- 'How can we set this up for success?' (people, budget, time: connects to priorities). Make the conditions for success so large that the others give up the idea.

- 'Why don't we do a full evaluation/test of this first to de-risk the idea?' By the time the evaluation is done, everyone will have moved on to the next bright idea anyway.

3 People:

- 'Who is this for?' (connects to priorities). If it is not for a powerful sponsor, question whether the idea can really succeed: urge the others to get a better sponsor, which they may find impossible.

- 'Who is best to do this?' (not me).

> Leaders know 'no' is a no-no.

Beyond the cheese shop

The ultimate form of resistance is to do nothing. Do not argue with or oppose the idea. Let other people take the heat for you. Only fight the battles you really have to fight. By doing nothing you create the one enemy that most corporates cannot defeat: inertia. There are so many other things going on that no one can find the time and energy to make the idea you dislike gain momentum. If the idea does gain momentum despite your doing nothing, you have plenty of opportunity to leap on board the bandwagon as it slowly trundles into motion.

> The ultimate form of resistance is to do nothing.

05
The partnership principle

Relationships within firms are a mess. We compete and cooperate with our colleagues. Increasingly, hierarchy is being challenged within and beyond the firm. Outside the firm it is clear that elites are no longer trusted or respected: the age of deference is over. Within the firm, staff are increasingly professional and well qualified: they do not take kindly to being managed by people they often see as being less able than themselves.

So how should we relate to our peers, and to people above and below us in the pecking order of the firm? As a leader, we need to reset the way we think. If we think in terms of hierarchy, then we land up defaulting to the parent–child script which is implicit in all hierarchies. The boss is the parent, who may be supportive or abusive, telling the child what to do. No wonder that people resent being managed.

In place of the parent–child script, we need to create the adult-to-adult script. Day to day, set aside the hierarchy and treat colleagues above, below and beside you as your partners. The hierarchy will re-assert itself at critical moments, such as pay and promotions. But day to day you can treat colleagues as partners. You may be above or below your colleagues in hierarchy terms, but that is irrelevant: you jointly need to achieve something and you both bring different capabilities to the challenge. Focus on capabilities, not power.

The partnership principle works wherever you are in the hierarchy.

Working with more senior leaders

If you act and look like a junior and inexperienced member of staff, that is how you will be treated. The classic symptoms are:

- talking too much and too fast (or sitting in dumbstruck silence);
- not dressing the part;
- fidgeting and looking nervous;
- being too eager to 'make your point' which you carefully prepared beforehand, but is completely irrelevant given the way the meeting has progressed.

If you want to be treated as a partner, you have to act that way. This requires a shift of mindset. You are not a junior person seeking an audience with a deity of the firm. You have a role to play which will ultimately help the CEO achieve her goals. You have something to contribute, so you are there for a reason. If you have the right mindset, the way you behave will change: behaviours are the symptoms of mindset. Here are the symptoms to check and the behaviour to work towards:

- Stay calm and focused.
- Listen and be ready to adapt to what you hear.
- Dress the part.
- Be clear about what you want from the meeting and what you can contribute.

Much of this comes down to preparation. Preparing for a presentation is easy: you are in charge of the script and it is mainly one-way communication. Preparing for a conversation is much harder. The conversation can go many different ways; you have to understand their agenda and needs; you need to be able to respond to many different scenarios and still get the outcome you want. And you need a back-up Plan B if Plan A is not going to work. But if you prepare well, you will feel confident and look confident. You will be halfway to acting like a partner, not a junior.

Working with less senior staff

It is easy to see why people resent traditional bosses. The classic symptoms are:

- talking, not listening;
- telling, not asking questions;
- being short and abrupt;
- ignoring staff members completely.

If you regard team members as partners, you shift your mindset. You realize that each person has something to contribute. As a leader, you need to find out how to get their best contribution. Each team member will have skills, knowledge and information to give. They will simply hear and see different things from you. You need everything that they can give. Equally, there is a huge amount they need from you: resources, direction, support, insight. Treat team members as partners and you start to build commitment, not just compliance.

You can treat your team as partners by doing the opposite of the traditional boss:

- Listen to your team, don't talk at them
- Focus on asking smart questions, not giving smart answers.
- Invest time with your team.
- Recognize what each team member can contribute.
- Value your team's contribution, don't ignore it.

This may look like common sense, but sense is rarely common in most firms. If you can do this, you will stand out and you will build a high-performing team.

> If you act and look like a junior member of staff,
> that is how you will be treated.

06
Negotiations

Principles

Negotiations are a fancy form of selling and decision making. They are often misrepresented as battles where one side wins and the other side loses. In practice, effective negotiations are based on two fundamental principles: 1) win/win; 2) focus on interests, not on positions.

The idea of negotiating is not to trick the other side. That ends up in a fight, which you might not win. Instead of competing, collaborate. All the greatest victories are won without a fight.

To succeed without fighting, find out what the other person wants to gain from the negotiation. The challenge is to think a little further than cost or price. Think through what the person's interests are, and focus the discussion on interests, not on positions. For example, a salary negotiation seems a classic win/lose argument. One side pays too much or the other receives too little. Working on interests shows a different perspective. The employer will want to retain talent. But there will be other interests as well: perhaps there is a new programme to be started or a challenging assignment to be undertaken. The employee is not interested only in money. The employee will be thinking about career development, work–life balance, assignments and risk and rewards in measurement and appraisal.

Based on this, there can be a productive discussion on what the employee really wants: how to balance work–life commitments, how much extra work, responsibility and risk he or she wants to take on, what skills the employee can develop and how much support and investment he or she should get (like money for training courses or sabbaticals). Suddenly, money becomes just one variable in a much wider mix. Both sides can now find areas of give and take and come to an outcome in which both sides feel they have had a win.

In a good negotiation, the language changes from a me/you discussion to a we/us discussion. You should both be working together to achieve a common outcome, rather than fighting each other.

Negotiating a partnership

The partnership should have been a marriage made in heaven. Hiro brought some great product to the table; Jayne had a great list of clients to whom she could sell. They were introduced to each other and success looked assured. Then it all went wrong. Hiro immediately focused on how much equity he should get for his product: he wanted over half because there would be nothing without him. Jayne wanted over half because Hiro would not be able to sell anything without her. We went back to basics.

What Hiro really wanted was money (of course, but that is different from equity), recognition for his achievements and the chance to create some more exciting products. He hated the idea of getting bogged down running a business. Jayne wanted to build a business with a portfolio of products and a real team supporting her. By looking at interests, the two sides realized they could work together happily: Jayne would sell Hiro's product, brand it under his name and give him an advance so that he could continue research work without the hassle of managing a business, and a royalty so that he could get rich if things worked well. Jayne kept 100 per cent of the equity. Both sides were happy: they got what they wanted.

All the greatest victories are won without a fight.

Process

By now you should be familiar with the sales process. Negotiations follow the same logical flow. The difference from selling is that you are working together to develop the logic; you are not simply pushing your own logic and solution. The process is:

1 **Agree the problem.** What is the common opportunity or challenge we can help each other with?

2 **Preview the benefits.** What are the positive outcomes for each of us? What are our interests, not just our positions?

3 **Suggest the idea.** In negotiations, you want to explore a range of ideas and possibilities: do not get locked into a single-point solution that invites a yes or no response. Create room for manoeuvre.

4 **Explain how it works.** Work this together so that both sides own the solution: this way, both sides will feel committed to it.

5 **Pre-empt objections.** Work together to identify the potential pitfalls and how you will overcome them.

6 **Reinforce the benefits.** Keep your eyes on the prize: this is why you are working together. And be very clear about what each side needs to deliver to the other side.

7 **Close.** Work out exactly what the next steps and responsibilities are, and then follow up.

This is rarely a single discussion.

> You are working together: you are not simply pushing your own solution.

Networks

Naive negotiators negotiate with one individual, hoping that he or she has all the power, authority, responsibility, time and goodwill to deliver the entire organization in support of what you are negotiating. Real life is not like that. Many negotiations depend on influencing a whole network. If you depend on only one person, you can depend on failure. It is up to you to identify and manage that network. Typically, there are six main roles in a negotiating network:

1 **Authorizer.** This person has the final decision-making authority and budget. You may only see him or her at the very start and end of the negotiations. Even if you are lucky enough to have this person as your main contact, he or she will still need your help in managing the decision-making network in his or her own organization.

2 **User/proposer.** This is often the person you will negotiate with on a day-to-day basis. This is the person with the immediate opportunity or problem, where you are part of the solution. Ideally, you will turn him or her into your coach (see below) so that you are jointly working to get the organization to support you. You want the user to be working with you, not against you: that requires understanding and respecting the user's real interests in the negotiation.

3 **Technical buyers.** These people must be satisfied that policies, standards and procedures are met. They are often in places like finance, HR, or health and safety. They cannot approve the proposal, but they can hole it beneath the waterline. These people are often ignored, which makes them dangerous. But involve them early, and they are often very helpful in clearing the way for you.

4 **Key influencers.** These people may not be obvious on any organization chart. They have informal influence, not formal authority, over decision making. They could be executive coaches, non-executive directors or senior non-line managers whom everyone trusts. Hunt them down: their opinions often carry weight because they are seen to be above the day-to-day political fray.

5 **Gatekeepers.** Gatekeepers provide or deny access to key decision makers. Secretaries are an obvious example. A good relationship leads to diaries becoming available; poor relationships mean the diary remains shut. Be careful of the executive who promises to get you access to the CEO or other senior leaders. This is often a

simple power play: 'Do what I want and I (may) get you access to the CEO.' You have just lost control, and the chances of gaining the access you want are still close to zero.

6 Coaches. These are people on your side who want to guide you through the decision-making jungle. There is always someone in the organization who will see value in what you are doing and will want you to succeed. The ideal is to turn everyone in the negotiating network into your coaches: they should see themselves as partnering with you, not negotiating with you. If you have properly understood their interests, they will normally be more than happy to help and support you.

EXERCISE 7.1   Influencing a network

These networks apply not only to sales situations. Try to map out the decision-making network for:

● a major project you are trying to push through;

● how your next bonus and promotion will be determined.

Now take the next critical step and identify for each person:

● What are their hot buttons: what will make them support me?

● What are their red issues: what concerns or limitations (time, money, power) do they have?

● What do I need to do next to bring them along?

Have one page per person, where you can keep track of contact details and each meeting you had with him or her, and the next steps. You will keep a complete map telling where you are and where you need to go to bring your project, promotion, proposal or bonus to a successful conclusion.

If you depend on only one person, you can depend on failure.

07
Networking

Breaking the ice

Some people love it, others hate it. Either way, you will have many opportunities to build your network within and beyond your organization. Most people flunk the opportunity. Watch what happens at conferences: people speak to people they already know, through shared geography, function or status. Very few people actually use the opportunity to extend their networks: people prefer to stay in the comfort zone of familiar faces. Leading from the comfort zone is not the road to success.

Networking is essential. Over 70 per cent of jobs are found through networking, not through headhunters or formal advertisements. Your career may depend on your network. Within your organization, you depend on networks to secure support for your assignments and to find your way to the next great assignment or opportunity.

Preparation is important. Know to whom you want to talk and why. Have a list of topics where you might want help and support: this will help you spot opportunities in the course of the conference or networking event.

A simple networking approach can be summed up as another alliterative three Es: engage, enthuse and enquire:

- **Engage.** Prepare some standard ice-breaking questions. Royalty uses: 'And what precisely do you do?' Get people talking about their favourite subject: themselves. They will like you for this. As they talk about themselves, you will find hooks to catch them with.

- **Enthuse.** Build rapport. You need to look for common interests: this could be work interests, pastimes or people you both know. Although enthusiasm is still a certifiable disease in the darker recesses of the Civil Service, the rest of humanity finds enthusiasm infectious (unless your enthusiasm is train spotting, in which case you have probably not put this book in your anorak to read on the station platform).

- **Enquire.** Find out what they are interested in, and where the common points of interest are. Do not try to negotiate a deal there and then: suggest that it might be worth getting together later to discuss the matter in more detail. Do not put them in a negotiating position: make sure you have built rapport and earned the right to follow up.

Next day, drop them an e-mail saying thank you and following up on any promise made.

> Let people talk about their favourite subject: themselves.

Building trust

There is a difference between knowing many people and having an effective network. An old-fashioned Rolodex full of business cards is not much use if no one returns your calls, or you find their diaries are mysteriously booked up whenever you want to meet them. You have to get beyond the ice-breaking stage promptly and start building a relationship.

Take care not to mistake alliances and business networks for friendship, even if you go out to company-sponsored social events together. Remember the dictum of Lord Palmerston, the 19th-century British prime minister, who said we 'have no permanent allies, only permanent interests'. In business, do not expect to have permanent allies, let alone permanent friends. Even your interests will change.

In this shifting and uncertain world, you need to anchor your relationships in mutual interest and mutual advantage. At the heart of building alliances is the need to build trust. Put simply: how far will you go to help someone you do not know or trust? In building alliances, think of the trust equation:

$$T = (V \times C)/R$$

An old-fashioned Rolodex full of business cards is not much use if no one returns your calls.

EXERCISE 7.2 Building alliances and trust

Create a shortlist of the people whose support you most need, including your boss. For each one, build a trust profile to see how well connected you are with them. Use the trust equation above, where: T = trust, V = values intimacy.

You share the same goals, same values, same priorities and same outlook. You do not need to like them. You both talk the same talk. You can start building trust fast here, even if you have not met someone before. The goal is to find some area of common interest.

Networking starts with the heart, not the head. Find ways to engage them emotionally. For example:

- Let them talk about themselves. Look interested. Flattery works.

- Find common colleagues ('Do you know so-and-so?').

- Find common business experiences to share: salespeople love swapping war stories, and so do most business people.

- Find common social interests.

- If you are meeting them in their office, look around for vital signs. Real examples include:

  - Pictures of lakes: 'How wonderful! Do you enjoy walking as well? In the Lake District? What a great place!'

– Professional qualifications on the wall: 'I see you got your degree from Harvard/Hull/Hamburg. What was that like?'

– A picture of a classic car: 'Is that yours? How long have you had it?'

For your own boss, you should be very clear about:

- How the boss will be measured and rewarded at the end of the year (his or her real interests).

- The three major projects the boss is working on this year.

- The boss's career ambitions, and how they will be achieved.

- The boss's personal interests, and whether any intersect with yours.

Once you have engaged the heart, you can engage the head. To make the network work, you need to find some common interests where there is mutual advantage to working together. Go back to the selling skills section (Part Six, Section 6): try to discover a common problem or opportunity to work on together, with clear benefits to both sides.

Back to our equation: $C = credibility$. This is the extent to which you have credibility with each other: have you delivered the results and fulfilled promises to each other? Trust building normally starts with small promises and obligations, and then builds up to larger ones. Credibility is about being able to walk the talk. Small things count. After a meeting, send a thank-you note or a summary of the meeting the same day. Speed impresses: it shows that you are both efficient and committed.

$R = risk$. We often think of risk objectively: financial risk, health and safety risk, litigation risk, political risk. This is important, but it is a sideshow in building alliances, trust and networks. Real risk is personal risk.

Look at risk from the other person's perspective: how will this affect me, how much will it cost me, how much effort will it take and will I look good or bad if it succeeds or fails? The more you can do to reduce the perceived risk and effort for someone else, the more likely he or she is to collaborate with you.

In building credibility, you will need to start on small and low-risk things so that confidence and credibility can build step by step. Ultimately, your network of alliances will be built one person at a time, one action at a time.

Networking starts with the heart, not the head.

08
Leading without power

In a traditional firm people have to follow you, because you are the boss. But now the people who rely on you do not have to follow you, because many of them will not be on your team. Instead, they have to want to follow you. That changes everything. You can no longer rely on command and control. You need to find ways of creating willing followers. This is where things go wrong fast for many leaders.

In the desire to be a popular leader, leaders try to be popular. This is logical, but fatal. Seeking popularity is a short cut to weakness. In the short term you will be popular, in the long term you will fail. This is the curse of all politicians in democracies: to gain power they have to be popular, but the need for popularity stops them being effective leaders.

If the currency of leadership is popularity, you will avoid all the difficult decisions and difficult conversations. You will not stretch people; you will stay in the comfort zone of business as usual; you will fudge and avoid performance issues in your team; you will not push back against other departments and teams when required. You will achieve a quiet life of underachievement. You will fail the leadership test of taking people where they would not have got by themselves.

If popularity is a false currency for leaders, so is power. You can no longer force people to cooperate with you. You cannot replace democracy with dictatorship. Nowadays, people have choices. If they do not like working with you, they will find alternatives. A leader with no followers is not a leader.

So if popularity and power are not the currency of leadership, what is the currency of leadership?

The new currency of leadership is respect. Respect is based on two vital ingredients: trust and positive challenge. Trust is dealt with extensively elsewhere in the book. As a reminder, you build trust through values alignment (you 'talk the talk' of the other person) and credibility (you always deliver on commitments, or you 'walk the talk').

Trust is good, but not enough for respect. As a leader you will gain respect with positive challenge. Set ambitious goals. These goals will stretch and develop your team, and give them a sense that they are achieving something meaningful. Ambition creates a sense of purpose and fulfilment. If you stretch people but do not support them, you are simply unreasonable. You need to make the challenge a positive challenge.

Positive challenge requires that you support your team. Set them up for success, and help and coach them as needed. If there are performance issues, deal with them positively. Help your team member step up. The process of positive challenge means that you have to have difficult conversations about goals, timing, resources and performance. They may be difficult conversations, but they should always be constructive conversations.

Build respect through trust and positive challenge and you will become the leader people want to follow, not the one they have to follow.

As a leader you will gain respect with positive challenge.

09
Managing upwards

Managing your boss

Most people assume that their boss manages them. Few assume the opposite: if you want to progress you have to manage your boss. In modern organizations, if you want to get things done, you have to make things happen through people you do not control: colleagues as well as your boss. Managing your boss is a core management skill.

As a simple test, write down the five things that you would want from someone working for you. Forget the formal evaluation systems. Focus on what you really expect. The chances are, that is what your boss wants from you. Here are five things bosses normally expect:

1 **Hard work.** You may think that you can get away with slacking or with presenteeism. But most bosses are not complete fools, despite appearances. They want a serious contribution from you, and that takes serious effort. They notice who puts in the effort and who does the minimum to survive.

2 **Initiative.** Don't wait to be told; don't expect the boss to provide all the answers. Don't delegate upwards. Take problems away from the boss, take initiative and help out. Drive to action, don't wallow in analysis.

3 **Intelligence.** Don't check your brain out at reception. Provide solutions, not problems. If you face a real challenge that you need to talk through with your boss, at least have some ideas of what a good solution might look like.

4 Reliability. Never surprise your boss, because surprises are rarely good. Set expectations clearly. If you can't do something, say so from the start. Once you have made a commitment, make sure you deliver on it. No excuses. And if things do go pear-shaped, make sure your boss knows early so that remedial action can be taken.

5 Ambition. Surprisingly, most bosses want ambitious staff. They want staff who will make the extra effort, who will solve problems, achieve results, make things happen.

Most boss problems come about because either there is a lack of trust or there is a clash of styles. In both cases, you can whine about the problem or you can do something about it.

Where you do not trust the boss, it may well be time to find another boss. But take care. The corporate carousel moves round with tedious regularity, and no boss lasts for ever. It is often best to wait for the carousel to turn and let your ways part naturally. And remember that you can learn from even the most dysfunctional bosses. There is normally a reason why they were promoted, something they are good at: learn those positive lessons while also learning about all the things you will do differently when you are in their position.

Where you have a clash of styles, your boss has no problem; you have the problem. Business is full of humanity and humans are different. Effective managers learn how to adapt to the style of the people they need to influence. You do not have to agree with the style of your boss; you have to adapt to it. If you can influence your boss successfully, you can probably influence anyone successfully. It is a skill worth learning.

Each boss is unique. In an unequal relationship, you have to adapt to your boss, because your boss is not likely to adapt to you. And given that bosses are unique, you have to understand not just their style: you have to understand their expectations. Everyone has a psychological contract with their boss, which is far more important than their formal employment contract. The essence of the contract is: 'You work hard for me and I will look after your career.' Some bosses are better than others at fulfilling this contract.

You have to understand what your boss really wants from you. How much initiative and risk should I take? How much should I communicate and when? What does the boss really want in terms of performance? How could I really screw up with this boss? None of this will be written down: you find out partly by talking to the boss, but also by talking to the rest of the team. Find out the reputation of the boss and act accordingly.

Finally, create some options. Make sure you network across and beyond the organization. You may need an escape route. By the time you need to escape, it is too late to start looking for the way out. If you have no alternative to your current boss, you are in a very weak position. At best you will have a benign patron. At worst you will be in a master–slave relationship, and you will not be the master.

Cardinal sins

There are an almost infinite number of ways to upset a boss. I once watched four security guards remove a marketing director from his office: one took hold of each limb and carried him out of the front door. His sin? He always walked through doors in front of the CEO, which made the CEO feel he was being upstaged.

Foibles and egomania aside, our research found a few common cardinal sins that bosses find difficult to forgive:

- **Disloyalty.** Disloyalty is by far the most unforgivable sin. Even the most demanding bosses tolerate occasional mistakes, bad jokes, bad dress and even bad performance. But disloyalty breaks the fundamental psychological contract between the boss and the team. Disloyalty is not just about bad-mouthing the boss. It is also about failing to support the boss and the team in a tight corner or failing to speak up when it is needed. If the team is to succeed, each team member must know that they can trust and depend on every other team member. When times are tough is when trust is most needed and is either built or lost fast.

- **Surprises.** Bosses don't like surprises. Don't hide bad news. Deal with it early; set expectations well.

- **Outshining, outflanking or outsmarting bosses.** Like you, your boss needs and wants to look good. Many bosses also have fragile egos. Do not try to steal their thunder. Help them. Good bosses will give you plenty of chances to shine.

- **Not delivering: unreliability.** Sometimes there are no easy short-cuts. Ultimately, you have to deliver, even if it is hard work.

- **Unprofessionalism.** This covers a multitude of sins. Keep careful note of the behaviour that pleases or annoys the boss. It can be small things like timeliness, who walks through doors first, who speaks up at meetings and when, dress codes, use or non-use of humour, and so on.

> Disloyalty is by far the most unforgivable sin.

10
Flattery

How many people think that they are overpaid, over-promoted and over-recognized? How many people think they are below average in terms of intelligence, honesty, diligence, trustworthiness, driving, loving and working? To have self-confidence we need self-belief: we have to believe that we are good. And yet most of us feel that we are under-recognized for our undoubtedly great talents and effort. And then someone comes along who recognizes our innate genius and excellence. Naturally, we will tend to think such a person has wonderful judgement, and we are likely to return the compliment when we can. In other words, when someone flatters us, we like it. Flattery works.

Research shows that there is no point at which flattery becomes counterproductive. You simply cannot flatter people enough. The more you flatter them, the more they like it. Flattery is an easy way to win friends and influence people. Here is how you can flatter people effectively:

- **Listen and empathize**. Just by doing this you flatter. Ask questions and let them talk about their trivial triumphs and travails. Be duly amazed by what they say; nod in agreement with what they say; empathize over the mountainous challenges they have had to overcome.

- **Praise in public**. Make the praise specific and personal: 'The way you dealt with that customer has shown us how we can turn a crisis into a triumph...'.

- **Seek advice**. Show how much you value the wisdom and insight of someone by asking for their advice. They will quietly purr with delight that they are being so respected.

- **Praise behind their back.** Spread praise to friends and colleagues of your target. The praise will get back to them and your stock will rise.

- **Contradict to conform.** Start with a contradiction: 'At first I did not see your point...' and then conform: 'but now I realize how right you were.' The initial contradiction makes the final conformity more credible and even sweeter to the listener.

There are a few ways to not flatter:

- **Avoid one-minute-management flattery.** 'Wow, you polished your shoes really well today.' At least try to make the flattery relevant and not demeaning.

- **Don't compete.** When your target is telling you their potentially very tedious stories about their challenges and triumphs, it is very tempting to match their story with your better and more compelling story. Avoid the temptation. You win by listening, not competing.

In any organization, it is better to win friends than to win battles. Once you have an army of allies, most battles melt away. You win without fighting. Flattery is a very cheap and effective way of winning the friends you need.

EXERCISE 7.3 Find out whose support you need

Identify the colleagues and bosses whose support you most need. For each one of them, identify:

- One thing you admire about them or have learned from them.
- One thing where they have helped you in the past.

Next time you see them, thank them for their help or compliment them about what you value in them. Repeat at regular intervals. Enjoy their reaction.

Part Eight
Financial skills

01
Managing budgets

You will not get promoted for managing your budget well. But you will get sent to the back of the class if you fail to manage it. Budgeting is a basic management discipline that has to be mastered. Here are the basics:

- **Negotiate a good budget to start with.** It is better to spend one month arguing furiously for a good budget than to spend 12 months trying to achieve a 'challenging' budget which has been set for you. If you have been set an impossible budget target, then no amount of good budget management will get you out of that dark hole. Start the year the right way. Use the techniques in 'Influencing decisions' (Part Six, Section 2) to get the budget settlement that will allow you to sleep at night, occasionally.

- **Follow the 48/52 rule.** Aim to achieve 52 per cent of your target in the first half of the year with 48 per cent of your budget. Now take your 48/52 budget for the first half of the year and do the same trick for the first two quarters of the year. This rule keeps you ahead of plan on costs and revenues (or outcomes). You want to be ready for any nasty surprises at the year end. The later the surprise comes, the harder it is to make up the difference.

- **Create some padding.** All good managers know how to create some flexibility for themselves. Play with the timing of hiring people: delay new hires, delay replacing team members. This automatically saves on salaries.

- **Get ready for the year-end squeeze.** There is always a year-end squeeze. Struggling departments will feel the heat from top management; other departments will have their budgets reset to adjust for the stragglers and stragglers. Adjustments are never in your favour. To get ready for the year-end squeeze you need to have padding and contingency in your budget. You also need to have some discretionary items you are ready to delay until the next year. And you must make sure that you have already spent any money allocated to discretionary items that are important to you (conferences, test markets, research, etc). If you have not spent on these items by the final quarter, you will find they get taken away from you in the year-end squeeze.

- **Work timings**. If you are having a good year, recognize costs early and delay revenue recognition. This means that you will not beat the budget by too much and your next year's target will not be too high; you will also have got next year off to a flying start with low costs and high revenues. On the other hand, if the year end looks tight, you need to find ways of deferring costs (put your annual team meeting back by four weeks and into next year) and, where possible, recognizing revenues as early as your auditors will allow.

- **Beware cost allocations.** Keep a lookout for other departments charging you and transferring costs to you. Head office is a big sinner here: they like to transfer as much of their costs out so that head office looks lean and mean, even if it is fat and bloated. Learn to say a very simple word: 'No'.

- **Stay on top of your numbers.** You should know all the critical numbers for your department, and you should be aware of any of the numbers going wrong. It is too late when you see the monthly management accounts. You need to spot in advance what costs and revenues are likely to be coming through and if there are any unwelcome surprises. If there is an unwelcome surprise, you need to take remedial action (find another budget item that can absorb the losses) and you need to communicate clearly what you are doing to your bosses. Budgets should never be a surprise, to you or to your boss.

Budgets should never be a surprise, to you or to your boss.

02
Negotiating budgets

How do you want next year to look like:

- Work exceptionally hard all year to meet a challenge goal? Get close and receive a modest bonus?
- Work exceptionally hard for one month a year to negotiate targets which you can beat relatively easily, and receive a big bonus as a result?

The simple leadership answer is that you be a Type A person: you should be an inveterate overachiever who will tilt at any windmill. But simple answers are not always the best answers. If you follow Type B you have two obvious advantages: the prospect of a better bonus and the prospect of a less stressful year. But there is a third advantage to Type B: you give yourself some spare capacity. If you are a natural underachiever you will reinvest any spare capacity in relaxation. If you are an overachiever, then spare capacity is your secret leadership weapon. Every new initiative, crisis or opportunity requires discretionary effort. It pays to make sure you have discretionary effort available to you over the year. The best way to do that is to work very hard for one month a year, when you negotiate your budget for the following year.

A budget is no more than a contract between different levels of management. The higher level wants to maximize the return and minimize the investment. The lower level wants the opposite: minimum commitment with maximum resource.

The principles of negotiating your budget are simple:

- **Strike early.** Anchor the discussion on your terms. This means setting expectations well before the formal budget process starts.

Once it starts, top management or planning will have set the broad framework and you are left simply negotiating the details.

- **Strike hard.** Marshal all your facts. Use facts like drunks use lamp posts: for support, not illumination. You are not trying to find the truth; you are making a case. You know more about your operations than anyone else, so even the most determined planner will give up in the face of a factual onslaught.

- **Strike often.** Keep on making your case. Don't let up. The reality is that top management and planners do not have the bandwidth to fight every battle. If you fight hard, they will find easier battles to fight elsewhere.

- **Build your coalition.** You need to strike the right contract with the CEO or top management. Remember it is a psychological contract as much as a budget negotiation. Cast your budget so that you are delivering to your CEO's agenda. But do not ignore planners and other influencers. Respect them, because otherwise they can make your life hard.

Over time you will learn all the tricks of the trade in managing budgets, such as:

- Don't overperform this year, because that just sets the bar higher next year. As a rule, the best predictor of next year's budget is this year's budget. So manage it well.

- Know where you can pad the budget: budget new hires for the whole year, but delay hiring them for a few months, for instance.

If you are the senior manager, then all of these rules are reversed. You will know all the tricks and you will have to manage them. The budget cycle can be a huge drain of time and effort, but it is vital on both sides to making sure that resources are allocated in the best way.

> A budget is no more than a contract between different levels of management.

03
Reviewing budgets

Budgets are like driving a car while looking in the rear mirror the whole time. You can see what has happened behind you, but you are unaware of a car crash coming towards you. This means that budget meetings can be a total waste of time: analysing the past, but ignoring the future. A good budget review is key to holding your team to account and driving your team to action. Here is how to make budget reviews work for you.

The budget is the budget is the budget. As the year progresses, you may see that variances are suddenly being measured against a re-forecast budget or some new benchmark. Do not let your team move the goal posts during the year. Once the budget is set, keep to it. This is a basic matter of accountability: hold each team member to account for the budget they agreed. They can only deviate from the budget if you agree explicitly to deviate.

A key variation of this is that you own all the cost savings. If costs are saved in one part of the budget, that does not entitle other areas to go over budget. You own the savings, and you decide if, when and where the savings can be deployed elsewhere.

Keep a consistent format. If the format changes every time you review the budget, you can never keep track of what is happening. A consistent format allows you to spot trends and spot variations. If the format changes, be suspicious: the chances are that someone is trying to hide something. People rarely try to hide good news. This means you have to work hard before the start of the year to make sure you have a usable format.

Look forwards, not backwards. The most important part of any budget is the year-end forecast. Ideally, this is the far right-hand column of the budget report. This tells you what your team expects to have achieved by the end of the year. The variances between year-end forecast and budget are the variances you need to worry about. Challenge these variances, and use them to drive to action: ultimately, you need to work on costs and/or revenues.

Looking forwards is the essential part of any budget review: turn the budget review into a budget preview.

Watch for accruals. Most budgets should be kept on an accruals basis, not a cash basis. Accruals are expenses which have been incurred, but which you have not yet paid for. For instance, your utility bill or an employee bonus will be due at the end of the quarter or year: cash accounting only recognizes when it is paid. Make sure that you really are accruing for costs which need to be accrued, otherwise you land up with a nasty shock when the bill finally becomes payable.

Spot the games. On the cost side, the budget will contain fat. Your job is to make sure you know where it is. This is your contingency fund for when things, inevitably, go wrong or you are required to improve your forecast outcome to make up for problems elsewhere in the firm.

On the revenue side, challenge revenues: make sure income is being recognized when it should be recognized. If 100 per cent of the value of a contract is recognized on signing, you have one bumper year of big high revenues and low costs, and then two years of high costs and no revenue.

> A good budget review is key to holding your team to account and driving your team to action.

04
Understand the nature of your costs

You have to understand the nature of your cost base. The core difference is between your fixed and variable costs. The balance between the two will drive your approach to managing the firm. High fixed costs make your profitability very sensitive to small changes in revenues, and also create barriers to competition. If all your costs are highly variable, it is easier to avoid huge losses but harder to make huge profits.

In the long run we are all dead, and in the long run no cost is fixed for ever. The difference between fixed and variable is about time horizon. A temporary worker with a flexible or zero-hours contract is more or less a completely variable cost; give that worker a full-time contract and they become much more fixed cost (subject to notice periods). Some costs are obviously fixed: the cost of rent on a building, where you are committed to a five-year lease is pretty much fixed. This makes retailing sensitive to small revenue changes: they pay the rent regardless of whether they sell anything.

Other fixed costs are less obvious, but equally important:

- **R&D.** If it costs £20 billion to design a new generation chip and build a plant for it, then that is a massive barrier to entry for other chip makers.

- **Marketing.** If the cost of running an effective national advertising campaign is £30 million a year, that gives a huge advantage to the competitor with the largest market share. The competitor with £100 million sales can afford the campaign, the competitor with £50 million sales has to get creative or get out.

IT costs are increasingly a huge fixed cost for banks, and much M&A (mergers and acquisitions) activity has been driven by reducing the fixed costs of IT and property: why pay for two bank outlets in the same high street? Why pay for two sets of IT systems costing £1 billion each, when you only need to pay for one?

The cost of a train or plane is fixed. The incremental cost of one more passenger is very small. And this leads to a massive trap. If it costs £10,000 to run the train, and each passenger costs only an extra £2 to serve, the temptation is to let prices drift down towards the marginal cost of £2; at £3, you are still making a contribution to the fixed cost of running the train. You need strong price discipline and effective yield management to ensure that the full costs of running the train are recovered.

Professional services firms are, in theory, variable-cost businesses where they bill clients by the hour or less. In practice, they behave more like fixed-cost businesses where the cost of the consultant is taken as a given: the goal is to maximize the revenue per professional. This drives long-hour cultures. Keeping a lawyer working late costs the law firm a pizza and a taxi ride, because a junior is on a fixed salary. It costs the client a fortune, and the partner makes a fortune.

Pharmaceuticals firms have huge and expensive sales forces which are largely fixed costs: mergers activity has been driven by the economies of scale of merging sales forces. Why have the costs of two sales forces when you only need the cost of one?

High fixed costs create the potential for scale economies and competitive advantage, but also require pricing discipline and effective yield management. Understanding costs is as important as understanding the market and competition in driving your strategy.

The core difference is between your fixed and variable costs.

05
Cutting costs

You have three approaches to cutting costs: the red dollars, green dollars and top dollars. To survive you need to understand red dollars and green dollars. To lead, you need to deliver top dollars.

Red dollars

The red dollar approach to cutting costs is smoke and mirrors. You promise gains, which let you survive without damaging your operations. It is game playing. Classic examples include:

- **Shifting costs from one bucket to another.** Reallocate costs internally or get customers to pay for what used to be free, such as help lines.

- **Focus on cash.** Delay payments to next year, bring forward revenue recognition. This stores up problems for next year, but it gets you through this year.

- **Bait and switch.** Make credible claims that you are saving money and that you are reinvesting it to protect quality, revenues, etc in another area. Most top managers stamp on this, but it can be worth a try.

Green dollars

The green dollar approach produces real savings. There is a natural progression to such savings:

- **Cut discretionary items.** This is the traditional squeeze on training, consulting, travel, entertaining and the coffee machine. If any discretionary items matter to you, buy them before the cost squeeze is imposed.

- **Sweat existing resources harder.** Delay replacing staff who depart for a couple of months; extend the replacement cycle on phones and computers. As the squeeze increases, ban overtime and put in a headcount freeze. Then raise the performance bar: be more demanding and ease low performers out.

- **Start the pain.** This starts with a hiring freeze. In theory this produces painless savings through natural attrition. In practice it causes chaos as the vital people leave from vital areas. When this does not produce enough savings, first offer voluntary redundancy and finally, enforce compulsory redundancy.

The green dollar approach is unsustainable: you are simply asking everyone to run faster and faster. At some point, they will collapse. The green dollar approach also is demoralizing. The cuts seem endless and so the best talent leaves. Only those who cannot leave remain. If you have to chase green dollars, then cut hard and cut once. The survivors need confidence that they have a future. Your team will not be committed if they think you might cut them at any moment.

Top dollars

The best way to cut costs is to do things differently. Stop running faster and buy a bicycle. Done well, you do not just focus on costs.

Change what you do. Start with your customers' needs and work back from there. This is the opposite of cost cutting which is internally focused. Cut out activities which do not deliver value to your internal or external customer.

Change how you do it; this is the world of re-engineering, methods change, outsourcing. Challenge everything and be creative.

This requires planning in advance and investing and changing the system while it is still working well. To do this you have to show real leadership by challenging complacency and orthodoxy.

By staying one step ahead of the crisis you never have the crisis. Prevention is better than cure when it comes to cost challenges.

The top dollar challenge is the leadership challenge: do more, do it better and do it for less. That requires changing what you do and how you do it.

The best way to cut costs is to do things differently.

06
Balanced scorecard

Financial management is vital but fatally flawed in two ways: it is backward looking and one-eyed. It reports on one aspect of the firm's health only. To understand the real health of your business you need a more balanced and forward looking health check: welcome to the balanced scorecard. It is a good way to monitor progress.

There are two versions of the balanced scorecard: the standard version and your version. Inevitably there are many versions of this, each jealously guarded by high priests who are convinced that they have the best version and that anyone using an alternative should be cast into hell. At the risk of incurring damnation, we will look first at a simplified standard version. It looks at four aspects of performance and progress:

- **Financial:** How have we performed and what is the likely expected financial performance?
- **Market:** Where are we with customers and competition?
- **Organizational health:** How effective are our management, sales and production processes? What is the status of our workforce skills, morale, development?
- **Learning and growth:** Are we innovating enough new products; are we improving our processes; are we developing our people well?

The good news *and* the bad news is that the balanced scorecard is a framework, not a prescription. It is up to you to decide precisely what you want to measure and how you want to measure it in each of the four main categories. The one which is routinely ignored is the fourth category: learning and growth. It is ignored because it is hard to measure how well we are preparing for the future, but arguably that makes it the most important measure. Assessing past performance (financial) or current performance (market and organization) is interesting, but will not make you great in the future (learning and growth).

You have to customize the balanced scorecard for yourself. If you want the right performance measures, start by throwing out all the measures you receive today. Start with a blank sheet of paper. Work out what you need to achieve over the next one to two years. Work back from there: identify what you need to do in order to reach your goal. Now you should have some idea of what you need to measure to ensure you reach your goal. Use the four elements of the balanced scorecard to push your thinking: if you are missing anything about internal processes or customers, for instance, think again.

Your performance template should sit on one piece of paper. You may well find that to start with you are missing about 50 per cent of the data you need and that you are receiving vast amounts of data you do not need. That is part of the point of the balanced scorecard: you can sort the signal from the noise in terms of measurements. You can focus on what matters. Once you know you have the right format, cascade it down through the firm so that each unit is finding data which can feed into your template. Inconsistent performance measures are nearly as useless as no performance measures.

Remember: what you measure is what you get in performance. Teams deliver what they are measured against. So make sure you measure the right things, and that is much more than finance.

EXERCISE 8.1 Build your own balanced scorecard

Start with a blank piece of paper and write down the information you really want in terms of:

- Financial performance;
- Market performance;

- Organizational and staff health;
- Learning and growth for the future.

Use this to drive performance and to force focus on the information you need to acquire.

You have to customize the balanced scorecard for yourself.

07
Making an investment case

Here are the six golden rules for making an investment case.

1. Focus on the assumptions, not the numbers

Investment cases are all about money and numbers, so it is natural to focus on these. But no one really believes the numbers. Everyone will assume that you started at the bottom right-hand corner of the spreadsheet with the desired outcome (plus some margin of error) and worked back from there. You will have rigged the spreadsheet to produce the 'correct' answer.

If the answer is rigged, the numbers are unreliable. So anyone looking at your spreadsheet will focus on the assumptions, not the numbers. Investment cases are not a numbers exercise: they are a thinking exercise.

2. Work the big assumptions first, and know how to justify them

Start with the big assumptions first: number of staff, average salary, market size and share, pricing. These are the things you will be tested on and you will have to prove that you have made sensible assumptions. Doubtless you will have made assumptions about how many paper clips will be used, but that will not change the direction of the business case. Focus on the big stuff.

3. Produce different scenarios

A single point projection is not credible because any plan does not survive first contact with reality. You will imagine scenarios in which everything turns out brilliantly well. The wizened executives looking at your proposal will see all the disasters which will lead to costs doubling and revenues halving. Understand what these risks are, how you can mitigate them and what the resulting outcome will look like.

4. An investment case which only just makes the grade is not worth it

Firms should only invest in projects which comfortably beat their investment hurdle, for two reasons. First, projected outcomes are rarely as good as achieved outcomes. So the project needs to start with plenty of head room. Second, from a portfolio perspective the firm needs highly profitable projects to offset all the failures, profit sinks and cash drains which the firm inevitably encounters. The firm cannot survive if its portfolio only has projects which at best can meet the minimum investment hurdle. Make sure your case looks like a winner, not a survivor.

5. Look at your case through the eyes of the buyer

Never fall in love with your idea. You may love your idea, but you have to understand how others will feel about it. Pitch your idea on the buyers' terms. In practice, this means two things:

- Follow whatever rules may be in place about making your case. There is huge debate about whether firms should use NPV, IRR, ROE, ROCE, payback or any other investment measure. The debate is irrelevant to you. Use whatever method has been prescribed, and then produce it in a format which is familiar to them. Make it easy for them.

- Understand their agenda: what do they want, and what do they dislike? Frame your proposal around their needs and wants, and their strategy. Talk their language to them.

6. Work the process

An investment case is not a purely rational decision. It is also a
political and emotional decision. So work the process. Politically,
build your coalition of support. Make sure that experts in each area
sign off on their part of the proposal, but do not give them power
of veto over the whole proposal. Gather as much intelligence as
possible about what the decision maker wants to see, and frame
your case appropriately. And work the detail: if necessary, make
sure your case is presented in a very polished fashion so that it feels
substantial. Other decision makers may just want a simple one page
note: give them what they want.

> An investment case is not a purely rational decision.

08
Understand your business drivers

In every type of business there are a few sacred numbers which drive the profitability of the business. Make sure you understand these numbers and how they work in your firm. A few examples will make the point.

Credit card firms

Profitability is driven by the NPV (net present value) of each card holder, This is driven by four variables:

- A: cost of **Acquisition**: are we using the most efficient channels to recruit card holders?

- S: average **Spend** and income per card holder: are we recruiting the right sort of card holder?

- L: **Loyalty**. This can be split into two metrics: do we achieve the right share of wallet; do they use our card or others, so do we have the right product proposition? Second, how long do they stay with us: do we manage retention of our card holders well?

- C: what is the **Cost** to serve our sorts of customers, including fraud and credit losses: do we have the right cost base, the right fraud and credit processes?

This sort of analysis allows you to look at NPV by type of sales channel, by type of customer and by type of product. Deep segmentation enables the credit card firms to discover who their best customers are and how best to target them. All models are an aid to thinking, not a substitute for thinking.

Retailers

Retailers have some simple metrics such as sales per square foot. But they all have the same underlying profit model for each store:

$$F \times E \times B \times S$$

- F: average **Footfall** passing by: are we in the right locations?
- E: percentage of passers by **Entering** the store: do we have the right market positioning to attract shoppers?
- B: percentage of people entering the store who **Buy**: do we have the right product range?
- S: average **Sale**/margin per buyer: are we able to sell the right product mix at the right price?

This is, of course, simplified. But a simple model helps you ask the right questions to drive the business forwards.

Other industries have simple but sacred numbers. Airlines look at yield: the average achieved price per available seat. Focus on that drives the pricing, sales and marketing models you see online where the airlines work hard to maximize revenue per seat. Hotels have a similar measure of yield per available room night. A bed in a hotel is like a seat on an airplane: once it is gone, it is gone and you cannot get any more revenue for it.

All of these metrics are simplistic. They are flawed in that they do not capture everything you need to manage such receivables, detailed budgets, capital structure of the firm. These models are not a substitute for all the rigours of detailed financial management. From a leadership point of view, you need to be able to simplify the challenges your team face and focus their efforts on the few things which will make the biggest difference. Do not get lost in the weeds of financial detail: focus on what matters most.

What are the numbers that drive your business? Find them and manage them.

EXERCISE 8.2   Build a simple financial formula

Build a simple financial formula for your business or unit:

- What are the key performance drivers for you to focus on?
- What are the magic numbers you need to focus on?

09
Managing pricing

Boxing champion Mike Tyson said: 'Everybody has a plan until they get punched in the mouth.' Having a pricing strategy or plan is easy; making it happen is hard. All the pressure from the market, and from your managers, is to reduce prices. Your challenge is to manage prices so that you can raise them, and to avoid a price war with competition which teaches your customers to buy on price only. If your product or service is similar to competition, you have a pricing challenge.

Here are some standard ways to optimize pricing:

- **Product variation.** There is a reason regulators like standard pack sizes: it makes price comparisons easy. Making price comparisons hard creates price flexibility. Mobile phone tariffs may seem to be a commodity, but once you have negotiated the whole package of phone model, minutes, data, texts, overseas calls, insurance, introductory rates, automatic upgrades and all the other variations on offer it becomes difficult to make a rational choice. A good salesperson will give you a story which lets you believe that you got a bargain, and lets them get their bonus.

- **Bait and switch.** Offer a very low-price product and then encourage switching to a higher-value offer. Food chains often do this: they advertise one cheap deal, and once the customer arrives try to get them to switch to a higher-price alternative.

- **Value progression.** This is a variation of bait and switch. Think of airlines: the basic flight may look cheap, but then you can choose all sorts of extras: checked baggage, reserved seats, special seats, priority boarding. Auto sales work the same way: a low base price leads to extras which are attractive to the client and profitable to you.

- **Inertia.** This is effective, common and unpleasant. Utility firms charge loyal customers most, keeping the best deals for new customers; airlines often may add extra charges at the end of the booking process. In both cases the producer is relying on the fact that the customer will not have the energy to start a new search process for a better deal. They penalize loyalty or idleness, depending on your perspective.

- **Hook and hike.** Hook customers with a low initial cost and once they are committed, hike the cost. This focuses on price and profit over the entire cycle and may involve an up-front loss to gain the client or contract. Examples include:

  - High-end consultants do an initial diagnosis at low cost, and sell in the full-price service when the client realizes the consultants own the problem and the solution.

  - Razors are sold cheap to hook the client into buying expensive razor heads. Aero engines are the same; the engine may lose money, but the profit is made on lifetime service.

  - Builders quote a low initial cost and once they are in find lots of unexpected problems which are costly to fix.

It is possible to get too clever with pricing, and especially with discounting. The achieved price counts, not the list price. The detergent maker may sell a product at £3 per unit, but then give the major retailer a volume discount, a feature allowance for in-store display, then there may be a customer discount coupon, a special promotional price and an allowance for advertising. Knowing the achieved price versus the list price is essential: elaborate discount schemes make it hard to know what your achieved price is and whether you are making any money.

Focus pricing on the achieved price not the headline price, and on the lifetime price not the initial price. Then be creative in presenting different price–value choices to your customers. Pricing is a creative process.

Pricing is a creative process.

10
Decoding CAPM

The capital asset pricing model (CAPM) is at the heart of modern financial theory. This is one reason modern finance is having a heart attack: CAPM is completely broken. But CAPM is like democracy, which Churchill described as the worst system of government, except for all the others. CAPM is the worst form of financial theory, except for all the others.

Whether you believe in CAPM or not, it is worth understanding.

The essence of CAPM is the idea that you should only invest in projects which yield a decent return. CAPM defines a decent return as the return you would get on a risk-free asset (such as a government bond) plus some more return for the extra risk you are taking on with your project. All of this makes perfect sense. Then you work the numbers in the model and the sense becomes nonsense.

Here is the formula for CAPM where the expected or required return is **Re**:

$$Re = Rf + \beta Rm$$

Watch how nonsense emerges from each term in the equation:

- **Rf.** The risk-free rate is decided by the return on government bonds. This assumes that they are risk free: you are 100 per cent guaranteed to get your money back. Ask people in Argentina how risk free government bonds are. And in the era of QE (quantitative easing) the return on government yields has been artificially supressed. In some cases, you end up paying the government to take your money. This is a weird and wacky world which is not a sound foundation for financial theory. Add in the challenge of terms: the risk-free rate varies depending on whether you take one-, five-, ten- or twenty-year bonds as your reference point. Your risk-free rate is, today, somewhere between 0 and 2 per cent.

- **Rm.** This is the risk premium on the market. Investing in stocks is more risky (in theory) than investing in government bonds. Some firms like Apple make a fortune for their shareholders; others go bust. On average, investors should expect a higher return for investing in stocks than bonds. The risk premium is a measure of how much extra return to expect. Estimates of the risk premium vary from roughly 4 per cent to 8 per cent if you look at historical returns in the UK and the USA. These historical estimates are deeply flawed: if you looked at stocks worldwide the risk would be much higher, as anyone who invested in Russian or German stock markets before their wars and revolutions would attest. Finally, the historical risk premium is inferior to the forecast risk premium. Without going through the formula here, currently that would yield a forecast risk premium of about 2 per cent.

- **β, or beta.** This adjusts for the risk of your specific project. A project which gets your suppliers to cut prices by 10 per cent might have zero risk. A project to mine for the elixir of eternal life in Pixieland might make you fabulously rich, but carries much higher risk. You would need a much higher return. There are ways of assessing beta for investing in firms, based on looking at beta over one or five years. But there is no reliable way of assessing beta for an individual project. Your score for beta could be anything from 0.001 for the supplier price cuts through to 1,000 for your Pixieland eternal elixir project.

Now let's put all the terms of CAPM together and see the nonsense emerge:

- **Rf:** somewhere between –0.5 per cent and 2 per cent, but utterly skewed by the effects of quantitative easing.
- **Rm:** somewhere between 2 per cent and 8 per cent.
- **β:** anything from 0.1 per cent to 10 per cent or more.

Plug those numbers into the formula and the required return on your project is somewhere between 0 and 82 per cent. In other words, you may as will pluck a number out of the air.

CAPM is well worth understanding, but not using. Understand it because it is part of financial literacy for any leader. Avoid using it because it is unhelpful. In practice, each firm will have its own way of assessing the financial viability of projects. Your firm's method is certainly flawed in theory, but that misses the point: it works in practice. As a leader, work with what works in practice, not in theory.

> CAPM is well worth understanding, but not using.

Part Nine
The art of strategy

01
Creating a vision

Creating a vision for teams

Visions are not just for mystics and chief executives. You do not have to be Martin Luther King and declare 'I have a dream' while standing on your desk. A vision for your team is much simpler: it is just a story in three parts:

1 This is where we are.

2 This is where we are going.

3 This is how we will get there.

Most of us can manage a simple story like that, on a good day. And if you want to make your vision motivational, you add a fourth element:

4 Here is your important role in helping us get there.

Note that the vision is not just about you. Make it relevant to each individual. People want to know they are doing something worthwhile, that their contribution is important and that success is possible. If your vision does these things, it will be powerful.

EXERCISE 9.1 Creating the team's vision

What is the 10-word vision for your department? How will you explain it to:

- your staff?
- other departments?

- management?
- customers?

Do you know what your boss's vision is and how you fit into it? What is your personal vision? How are you going to get there?

People want to know they are doing something worthwhile, that their contribution is important and that success is possible.

Creating a vision for the whole organization

When creating a vision, remember RUSSIA – it represents the six elements of a strong vision:

1 Relevant. The vision should be relevant to the current context and challenges of the organization. It should also be made relevant to each stakeholder in the organization.

2 Unique. You could not (easily) substitute the name of any other organization into the vision: it is unique to the strengths and aspirations of the one organization.

3 Stretching. The vision should be more than business as usual. It should have an element of stretch in it. This will help managers understand priorities and focus their efforts: it will help them understand what they should do and should not do.

4 Simple. If a vision is not simple, it will not be remembered. And if no one remembers your vision, it is unlikely that they are going to be able to act on it.

5 Individualized. Everyone in the organization should feel they have an important role to play in helping to achieve the mission.

6 **Actionable**. A vision that is not actionable is a pipe dream. You have to turn the idea into action. You need a clear goal and the means to achieve the goal.

A classic vision: NASA

John F Kennedy famously announced a mission 'to put a man on the moon and bring him back alive again, by the end of this decade'. This was the mission impossible that led to the creation of NASA. On 16 July 1969, mission impossible was accomplished.

Let's put the NASA vision to the RUSSIA test:

1 **Relevant**. This was about beating the Russians in space: the Russians had already put the first satellite into space (*Sputnik*) and the first cosmonaut (Yuri Gagarin). The United States was losing the Cold War in terms of technology, prestige and the race for the last frontier. It was a must-win battle for the nation.

2 **Unique**. It would be hard to claim that a moon landing was the vision for Procter & Gamble or Shell: it was a truly unique vision.

3 **Stretching**. At the time, no one knew if the vision was possible or if the technology could be developed: it was a huge stretch.

4 **Simple**. Everyone could remember it. The power of the vision was compelling: it galvanized political, financial and technical support. It kept NASA focused so that setbacks like some of the *Gemini* disasters did not destroy the programme. Then look at what happened when the vision was achieved: NASA lost its way. It may have a vision now, but not everyone knows it. It has had some successes (the Hubble telescope) but the setbacks tend to set it back a long way (the shuttle disaster).

5 **Individualized**. In a space mission, everyone's role is important. If the smallest detail goes wrong, disaster ensues, as the *Challenger* tragedy shows.

6 **Actionable**. There was a clear goal and NASA created the means to achieve the goal. It was actionable and it was put into action.

Now compare your organization's vision with NASA's: does it have
the RUSSIA values of NASA pre-1969 or post-1969?

EXERCISE 9.2   Creating the organization's vision

Create a 10-word vision for Microsoft's shareholders and
employees, for example. Create another 10-word vision for
Microsoft's regulators and customers.

Test your company's vision against the criteria above.

Create a 10-word vision for your company, again looking at how it
might alter for different stakeholder groups.

If a vision is not simple, it will not be remembered.

02
Classical strategy

Everyone thinks they know what strategy is, until you ask them. Then you find that everyone has a different definition of what strategy really means. In practice, the idea of strategy falls into two broad camps: the classical and the post-modern. This section discusses classical strategy, and post-modern strategy is discussed in Section 3.

Classical strategy is deeply analytical, which suits the pointy heads in the main strategy consulting firms. They will analyse your market, customers and competition so that you can find a way of winning. At least, they will help you survive long enough to pay their fees. The patron saint of the analytical school is Michael Porter, who came up with the five forces approach to analysing the market. It is worth knowing this framework, because it gives a useful way of thinking about the position of your firm:

1 **Internal rivalry.** This is about the power of your existing competition. Do they have a lower cost base, scale economies, better brands, higher market share, deeper pockets for a price war?

2 **New entrants.** How secure are you from new entrants invading your space? Patents, regulation, strong branding, network effects, scale economies all make it harder for new entrants to break in.

3 **Substitutes.** This looks at how you define your market. Customers may think about going out to see a film in the evening, but decide instead to save some money and get a pizza delivered: pizza and cinema tickets are substitutes which compete with each other. Pepsi and Coke are clear internal rivals, but they are both

competing for share of throat: so they are competing with other soft drinks, tea, coffee and water. They may choose to expand into all those categories.

4 **Buyer power.** If you depend heavily on one or two major buyers, you will be squeezed. Suppliers to large retailers often find themselves in this bear hug. The retailer gives a supplier a big break, which lets them grow, the supplier then becomes dependent on the retailer who starts the big squeeze on prices and margins.

5 **Supplier power.** This is about your dependence on a supplier for key inputs, which may be technology or know how. For instance, franchisees are at the mercy of the franchisor for the existence of their business. They may thrive, but they do so on the franchisor's terms.

The Porter analysis shows how attractive your business is, at a high level. Further analysis will show how well positioned you are within your market. This is where the venerable BCG (Boston Consulting Group) Grid comes in. It compares the attractiveness of the market with your market posiition and makes predictions and prescriptions accordingly:

- **Growing market/high share.** Stars: great prospects, great business. Probably cash neutral: high investment required, but achieving high returns. Keep and grow.

- **Growing market/low market share.** Dilemmas: could have great prospects, but will require heavy investment to succeed. Double or quits strategy: invest or sell.

- **Declining market/high share.** Cash cows: poor long-term prospects; needs low investment, returns cash to help you invest elsewhere. Keep it and milk it for cash.

- **Declining market/low share.** Dogs. Consuming cash, no prospects. Get out.

Even where you use conventional analysis, be ready to use unconventional insight. Figure 9.1 presents a classic portfolio analysis based on the BCG matrix.

Figure 9.1   Portfolio analysis

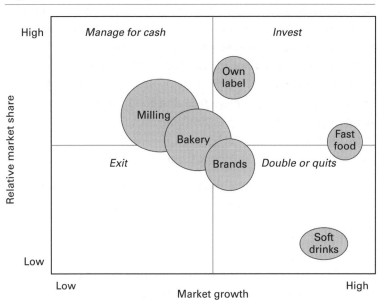

A few challenges are immediately apparent:

- Most businesses cluster in the middle of the graph: they do not yield easy answers.

- It is not clear what is a separate business: milling supports baking which supports own label and brands: how separate are they?

- What really is the market share of the soft drinks business: is it share of all drinks from coffee to cola to water? Or is it just the direct competitors in each local market?

Reality is never as simple as it is presented at business school. Even if you succeed in pinning the businesses on the matrix, should you follow the normal prescriptions, which would imply:

- Managing the large milling and baking businesses for cash as their markets slowly decline.

- Investing heavily in the growing fast-food markets to secure the future.

That is probably the worst strategy possible. Everyone else in the industry was doing the same analysis and coming to the same conclusions. All the weaker millers and bakers just wanted to get out of the business: their operations were for sale at bargain prices – if you have deep experience in making milling and baking plants work well, that is a huge opportunity to consolidate the industry. Meanwhile everyone was desperate to expand their fast-food businesses and would pay a big premium to snap up any other fast-food business.

So the best strategy, which saved the firm, was to do the opposite of what the strategy framework suggested:

- Invest heavily in milling and baking, buy rivals at discount prices and optimize their plants.

- Sell fast-foods business at a big premium, to release cash to invest in milling and baking.

You can analyse the past, but you cannot analyse the future. You can imagine the future and as a leader, you can create the future. Over to you.

Classical strategy is important because it brings intellectual rigour to strategy, as opposed to relying on gut feeling. The problem is that the analysis is rarely clear cut, and the prescriptions may be unhelpful. Looking at the great business successes of the past 20 years, it is hard to find any which have been driven by traditional analysis. Every great start up does not start with a Porter analysis: it starts with a dream. These dreams often turn into nightmares for the incumbents who see their industries overturned by newcomers who break all the rules.

Clearly, there is another form of strategy which makes a difference.

EXERCISE 9.3   Conduct a Porter analysis

Conduct a Porter analysis on your business:

- What is the power of your existing competitors relative to you?

- Who are the new entrants and are they changing the rules of the game?

- How strong are your customers – do you rely on a few or many?
- How strong are your suppliers – do they control vital resources such as technology, intellectual property, access to finance?
- Are there any substitutes to your product or service which could make you irrelevant?

EXERCISE 9.4   Conduct a simple SWOT analysis

Conduct a simple analysis of your prospects: for you, your unit and your business. Do a SWOT analysis: Strengths, Weaknesses, Opportunities and Threats. It may be simple, but it is effective:

- What are the strengths of your business which you can build on?
- What are the weaknesses which hold you back?
- What are your main opportunities: markets, customers, technology, products, etc?
- What are the threats you face from competition, regulation and other changes?

Classical strategy is important because it brings intellectual rigour to strategy, as opposed to relying on gut feeling.

03
Post-modern strategy

Classical strategy works for incumbents in relatively stable industries. It does not help entrepreneurs much: the analysis would tell them that they have no chance of succeeding against well entrenched competition.

There is an alternative. Classical strategy is all about designing the solution. Post-modern strategy is all about discovering the solution, and breaking all the rules as you go along. Classical strategy works for incumbents and legacy firms; post-modern strategy works for new entrants and disrupters. Occasionally, legacy firms aspire to being post-modern: the effect is the same as watching Granddad going clubbing.

The patron saints of post-modern strategy are CK Prahalad and Gary Hamel, supported by people like Chan Kim. Where classical strategy appeals to the head, post-modern strategy appeals to the heart. The essence of post-modern strategy is to change the rules of the game so that they suit you. Some of the themes you will hear them talk about include:

- **Strategic intent.** Have a clear, outrageous ambition. Komatsu when it started out set the goal of Maru-C: encircle (and kill) Caterpillar.

- **Core competence.** Slowly build the skills and capabilities which your competitors will find hard to copy. Examples include Honda, building expertise in engine technology, in which they can compete.

- **White spaces/blue ocean/segment retreat.** The best way to win a battle is without fighting: find areas where your competition is absent. The classic example is Canon developing small photocopiers to take on Xerox which dominated technology for the print room. Similarly, Komatsu started with small diggers, which suited many Asian markets but were beneath the dignity of Caterpillar engineers who liked building big diggers.

- **Expeditionary marketing.** This is the essence of post-modern strategy. You cannot tell what customers will want in the future: you have to discover it. The best way is to prototype like crazy and test the ideas in the market. Learn from the failures and withdraw them fast, invest heavily in the successes. The Japanese soft drinks industry is a frenzy of non-stop innovation.

- **Value innovation/value curves.** At its simplest, draw up a list of what your customers most want, then design your service around that, and eliminate all expense which does not add value. This harks back to the original concept of process re-engineering, which was very customer led. The classic example is Formule 1 hotels, which achieved very low price and high satisfaction by delivering only what guests want: a good bed in a quiet and clean room.

There is a reason why post-modern strategy works for innovators, not incumbents. New entrants can only succeed through asymmetric competition: they have to change the rules. This presents a challenge for incumbents: if they change the rules, they just cannibalize their own business.

Post-modern strategy is about changing the rules of the game in your favour. If you fight by the rules of a large incumbent, you will lose. Change the rules in your favour and you will discover that a great idea beats the dull weight of money every time.

> Post-modern strategy is about changing the rules of the game in your favour.

04
Strategic discussions

At some point in your leadership career, you will need to engage in serious strategy discussions. At first, these discussions can seem very theoretical and remote from your day-to-day reality. But these discussions are vital: they will determine how the firm allocates its resources, where its priorities will be, what businesses it will be in and how it will compete effectively. You need to be at the table when the discussion happens, and you need to influence it well.

The art of strategy is as much about asking smart questions as it is about finding smart answers. Top strategy firms interview candidates using cases: they do not expect the interviewee to know all the right answers, but they do expect them to know all the right questions. You can only find the right answer if you know the right questions. Here is your guide to asking the right questions:

- **Customers**. Who are our customers? What is the value of the market? Is it growing or declining? What do they want? Are there different segments with different price/value expectations? How well do our offerings match their value expectations? What is our value proposition? Are there any under-served or ignored needs or customer types? Who are our most loyal customers and why? What can we learn from customers who switch to us or away from us?

- **Competitors**. Who are the existing competition and what are their relative strengths and weaknesses? What is our relative market share, and are we gaining or losing share? Why? Can we create barriers to entry through technology, scale, brands, other? Do we have a source of unfair advantage? How can we change the rules of the game to our advantage?

- **Channels.** How do we go to market? What are the cost and effectiveness of different channels: direct, distributors, wholesalers, etc? What alternatives exist?

- **Financial.** Where do we generate or use cash? Where are the profit sanctuaries of our competitors and can we wreck them? What are the economic drivers of our business: utilization, scale?

- **Operational.** How effective are we: do we deliver the right sort of value, or are we spending on things which customers do not need? How efficient are we, compared to competition and potential? Are we organized the right way: what are the things we need to do ourselves, and what can we outsource or offshore to partners who can do it better or cheaper? Do we have the capacity to learn, grow and innovate? What should we be innovating?

A good strategy discussion will start with the market and with the customer. If you do not understand your customer you will not know how to compete or how to survive. These questions need to be probing: do not assume that today's customers and today's needs will be tomorrow's customers and tomorrow's needs. In the words of Bill Gates: 'We tend to overestimate the amount of change that will happen in two years, but underestimate the amount of change which will happen in ten years.' But by the time you see the world is changing, you are too late. You have to anticipate change, not just react to it.

> Do not assume that today's customers and today's needs will be tomorrow's customers and tomorrow's needs.

05
Competitive strategy

If you think your firm has a competitive advantage, move firms. Most competitive advantage is weak. Here are some classic forms of weak advantage:

- **Price** (which competition can copy in minutes), unless you have a fundamental cost advantage (scale economies, or a reworking of the value/cost trade-off). Price advantages can be copied, some cost advantages cannot be copied.

- **Service.** You may think you offer better service but what do your customers think and how easily can you be copied?

- **New widgets.** You design a great new product, but can it be patented? Is there anything to stop competition learning from your mistakes: can they introduce a better product on the back of your R&D and market effort?

How competitive is this advantage? The hotel was reviewed on TripAdvisor as the 'Best of Bland'. This was meant to be a compliment: the hotel had worked out the formula for serving business travellers, and delivered it. That is good. But the formula is universal, so when you step into one of these hotels you could be in Beijing, Boston or Berlin. And you could be in any one of several chains. The hotel manager threw a strop. He was convinced that his hotel's service set it apart from all others. This was his unique source of advantage. It was not: seen through the customer's eyes service was exactly what you would expect from such a hotel. We often kid ourselves about how strong our competitive advantage is. Customers are not fooled; see the world through their eyes.

Instead of competitive advantage, build a source of unfair advantage. The problem with a fair fight is that you might lose it. Only fight when you know you can win. We all believe in the rhetoric of markets and competition, provided we win. The most successful firms have a source of thoroughly unfair advantage:

- **Oil and gas:** access to the lowest-cost oil and gas fields.

- **Pharma firms:** patent protection for blockbuster drugs.

- **LinkedIn, Facebook, SWIFT:** network effects where the value of the service rises with its reach, making it very hard for new entrants.

- **Natural monopolies:** utilities like gas, water and electricity distribution are natural monopolies. There is not much point in trying to provide two sets of water mains to each house.

- **Access to key resources:** television sports rights are a unique resource which generate significant premiums (but supplier power means that the sport extracts most of the economic rent from this).

- **Retailers:** access to the best locations.

- **Consumer goods:** strong brands are unique and command a premium: Apple, Mercedes Benz, Ferregamo, for instance.

A simple (but not infallible) way of testing the strength of your competitive advantage is to look at your profitability. If you are earning the sorts of margins that drug barons dream of, then either you are a drug baron or you have a source of thoroughly unfair competitive advantage, which you can use to maximize your economic rents. If you have marginal profitability, the chances are that you have a weak competitive advantage. But at least you are unlikely to be a (successful) drug baron.

> The problem with a fair fight is that you might lose it.

06
Understanding the customer

Why do people buy one product instead of another? If you understand this mystery, you are well on the way to success. Buying is both a rational and an emotional decision. You need to tap into both sets of motives. You can think of why people buy at three levels:

1 **Features.** Every product has features such as price, size, components. Some people wax lyrical about double overhead camshafts on cars: they are a feature of the car. But most people do not buy on the basis of features, however exotic they may be.

2 **Benefits, which appeal to the head.** This is what the product or service will do for you. Economists would have you believe that we are rational beings who buy on explicit price/benefit trade-offs. But that does not explain why people buy apparently frivolous purchases like luxury cars, bags and clothes when cheaper alternatives do the same job.

3 **Hopes and dreams, which appeal to the heart.** What we buy and do is not just a rational choice: it defines what we do, who we are, how we see ourselves and how we want to be seen.

Effective marketing taps into all three levels. Overtly, you will always be selling to benefits: the features of your product give buyers a reason to believe that you really can deliver the claimed benefits. The most effective marketing hooks into a deeper sense of identity: people want to be associated with your product or service.

Table 9.1 Features, benefits, hopes and dreams

	Features	Benefits	Hopes and dreams
4×4 off-road vehicle	High driving position. Large engine.	Good visibility. Goes anywhere.	Status. Be an adventurer.
Fitness monitor and watch	Heart rate monitor, GPS.	Shows how well you are exercising and resting.	Be healthy. Show friends and colleagues what you are like.
Disposable nappies	Extra-absorbent layer. Cuffed legs.	Dry baby. No leaks.	Happy baby, happy mother.

An extreme example is Fairy liquid, which is a popular and upmarket dishwashing liquid in the UK. It claims two distinct benefits: it lasts longer than rivals (so it is worth the premium) and it is gentle on the hands that wash the dishes. So far, so boring. But there is a curious feature of Fairy liquid. Travelling around blue-collar estates, about half the households had a bottle of Fairy liquid in the kitchen window, above the kitchen sink. If there was no Fairy liquid, there was no rival to be seen. What was going on? Fairy liquid overtly sells benefits. Implicitly it sells a hope and a dream: if you are house proud, you spend a bit extra and use Fairy Liquid. If you are not house proud, you use a cheap alternative. So for a few pennies extra, you can show all your neighbours that you are house proud. If even dishwashing liquid is selling a hope and a dream, then anything has a hope and a dream in it.

Marketing to hopes and dreams is not just about retail consumers. It also applies in the business-to-business world. Never forget that we are all heroes of our own life stories. Each buyer you deal with is their own hero, fighting their own heroic battles: you are a bit-part player who can help them remain a hero by helping them achieve their goals. You can also reverse this: the dark side of hopes and dreams is fears and nightmares. If they make the wrong decision, they will be seen as the office idiot. If you can be the safest alternative, then you can charge a real premium for that. No one gets fired for hiring McKinsey, and if their advice leads to ruin, at least you can claim you did all that was possible.

Finally, remember that not all customers are the same. Talk of the average customer is useless. The average human is 51 per cent female and has slightly less than two legs (some people have lost legs). That is 100 per cent useless information. Instead of looking at the average, look at different groups, or segments, of customers. If on average customers score your product 3 out of 5, that tells you nothing. If you then find some score it zero out of five and others score it 5 out 5, that is very valuable. The people who love your product create a very valuable market for you, and you can ignore those who hate it because they will never buy it.

> Talk of the average customer is useless.

Marketing strategy

Traditionally, there have been two sets of alliterations which describe the main elements of a marketing strategy:

- The four Ps: Product, Price, Promotion and Place.
- The three Cs: Customers, Channels and Competition.

Curiously, the four Ps make no mention of profits and the three Cs make no mention of costs. Those may be omissions which indicate why marketing executives often do not get the recognition or promotion which they believe they deserve.

These checklists are useful to make sure you are asking the right questions about your marketing strategy. You will note that the marketing strategy has heavy overlap with corporate strategy. For an individual line of business, a good strategy starts with the market.

The checklist raises the right questions, but the challenge is to find the right answers. Most discussions about marketing or corporate strategy are elaborate ways of justifying what we already do, plus or minus a bit. That is a fatal rut to fall into: you leave yourself open to competitors who are more innovative, work harder and are more creative.

This means that the strategy process is vital, not just the strategy questions. Here are three ways to keep the strategy process on track.

Defend what you have

Gaining new markets and new customers is risky and expensive. As a rule of thumb, it costs seven times as much to acquire a new customer than it does to sell to an existing customer. Existing customers buy more than new customers. Relentless focus on defending and building on what you have is vital: you can learn from existing customers about emerging needs, trends and competition; they give you economic scale and a strong reference base; they produce the profits which support all your new ideas, R&D and test markets. Before you let your team imagine a successful future, make sure they deliver a successful today.

Understand what customers really want

In theory, this is the world of market research. As ever, the answers you get depend on the questions you ask and how you ask them. Here is what to consider:

Quantitative surveys

Quantitative surveys will tell you how big the current market is and where the main opportunities are today, and what the major market trends have been in the past. But they do not open a window to the future. Also, beware the curse of averages. On average, humans are 51 per cent female and have slightly less than two legs. Useless information. The real interest is often in the outliers: the heavy users and disloyal users. Understand them and you may gain real insight.

Qualitative research

Qualitative research is useful for insight, but carries two risks. First, the insight may not be representative of the market as a whole. Second, opinions are not the same as behaviours. Everyone agrees that healthy eating is a good thing; not everyone eats a healthy diet. What customers say and do may be quite different.

Behavioural research

Behavioural research is difficult, time consuming and expensive. You have to find ways of observing actual or potential customers using or buying your services or those of your competitors. But done well it will give you real insight into what customers need and value, how you compare and how you might improve in the future. At minimum, try being a mystery shopper of your own services. If airline crews had to endure the same airport misery of rubbish check-in, security, passport control and baggage retrieval as they inflict on their customers, then we would suddenly find that airport misery would be a thing of the past. When you insulate yourself from your customer experience, you have no idea what they go through, and you have no incentive to improve. Until a new competitor enters and puts you out of business.

Identify customers' future wants

Identify what customers will want in future. The customer may be right, but often does not know what they want. They cannot tell you what they will want in future. You need to get creative about imaging the future for your customers. Fortunately, there are ways of being creative even if your name is not Picasso. Here is how:

- Live or work with your customers as they use your services: see what they do, where they struggle and what they do not use. Re-engineer what you offer around what they need and strip out everything else. If they have a problem, find a way of solving it and you will be a hero.

- Talk to your heaviest users and to customers who deserted you. These outliers will give you great insights into what you do best and worst or not at all.

- Copy someone. This is the easiest way to innovate and see the future. Someone, somewhere, in a country far, far away is already creating the future. They are doing something highly innovative that works. Keep close to your customers and suppliers; keep listening and when you hear of a great idea, be ready to jump in and copy it (where this is legal...).

- Try something. The best way to find out what works is to try it. This is easier with some things than others. You cannot just 'try' a new nuclear power station or a new chip fabrication plant costing £20 billion or more. But you can quickly create prototypes and test new offerings online; you can quickly test market acceptance of new recipes for supermarket foods. Learn how to do this fast and at low cost so you can learn and innovate faster than anyone else.

> The answers you get depend on the questions you ask.

08
Pricing strategy

Many managers are weak at pricing management. They avoid raising prices where possible: the easy way out is to cut prices and keep customers happy. But you cannot cut your way to success. Success requires investment in products, services, people, marketing, channels and partners. You need price discipline to succeed.

Pricing discussions start in the wrong place: they start with price. Instead of starting with price, start with value. Your pricing power is determined by the value you add. The value equation is very simple:

$$Value = quality - cost$$

Using the value equation, both McDonald's and the Ritz provide value, but with very different price points and quality points. This means that when a manager resists a price increase, they are in effect saying that they have no confidence in the quality and value of what you are delivering. The solution may not be to reduce price, but to increase quality. Lowering prices is easy, but fatal:

- Price cuts are a zero-sum game: your competitors can cut prices on the same day you cut yours. So you gain no advantage.

- By cutting prices even for a promotional period you train your customers to expect lower prices and to hunt for bargains.

- You make your product or service a commodity and it becomes very hard to raise prices again.

Price cutting is the lazy way to ruin, normally.

Start your price discussion by talking about quality and value, as seen from your customer's perspective. The need for lower prices is the same as the need for higher quality and value. Price reduction only makes sense competitively where:

- You are the lowest-cost producer and price reductions will force others out of the market.

- You need to build scale fast to achieve network economies: many online businesses have real network economies. Facebook or Skype would not be of much use with just one user: the more users sign up, the more it becomes attractive to all users.

- You have strong economies of scale or have a steep learning curve to exploit: either way, you may reduce prices in anticipation of being able to reduce your costs, so that you squeeze competition.

Customer value may determine the ideal price target, but there are two other constraints on pricing:

1 **Costs.** If costs exceed price, you have a cost problem and a value problem.

2 **Competition.** The market will enforce price discipline at some point. If you are too greedy, you simply invite new competitors and strengthen existing competitors by allowing them to follow you in charging high prices.

Costs, customers and competition all impose pricing discipline. But in each case, the discussion should come back to value:

- **Customers:** are we adding enough value to justify raising prices?

- **Costs:** are we spending money which does not add value and do we need to invest more in where we can add value?

- **Competition:** how can we add more value and charge more than our competition?

Focusing on the value question produces better answers than focusing just on the price question.

EXERCISE 9.5 The value questions

- What is the value your customers get from your product or service?
- Are you offering any features which your customers do not value highly? Can you cut those features out and save money?
- What is the value you deliver compared to competition and substitutes, and at what price? Can we add more value and charge more than competition?
- Are there incremental services which customers value and which cost us little to deliver?

Your pricing power is determined by the value you add.

09
Dealing with advertising

Everyone thinks that they are an expert at advertising. We all see lots of advertising every day, and we know what we like and do not like. So we must be experts, right? Wrong.

Advertising is not about what we like or not. It is about what will persuade people who are not like us to change their behaviour, change their thinking and buy our products. If you know how to change the way strangers think you will not just understand advertising; you are a genius who will make a fortune in myriad ways.

At some point you may need to deal with an advertising agency, or at least with your marketing director. You will need to know how to have an intelligent discussion about advertising without reverting to 'I like this' and 'I don't like that': opinion is no substitute for insight.

Here are some simple and universal tests of good advertising:

- Does it meet our advertising brief (strategy)? (See the following section.)

- Is there a clear promise? What are we promising to the customer, and is it clear and simple? If we promise two things, that is one thing too many.

- Is it relevant? Does it deal with a real customer need?

- Is it credible? Does the advertising give people a reason to believe that we can deliver our promise?

- Is our product or service the hero of the advertising? If you have a celebrity to front your campaign, the danger is that everyone remembers the celebrity, not you.

- Is the advertising consistent with the character of our brand, product or service? If we want to be seen as exclusive or clinical and efficient, or friendly and helpful, does that character come across?

- Is it unique? If we substituted the name of our main competitor into the advertising, would it make sense? If it does, then we have not got a unique offer.

If you ask these questions relentlessly, you will not gain popularity but you will gain respect. Your marketing director and advertising agency may want to do something funky and creative which will win advertising awards. You do not need creativity: you need impact. You do not need to win industry awards, you need to win customers. Move beyond what you may like and focus on what works.

> You do not need to win industry awards;
> you need to win customers.

10
The advertising brief

Clients get the advertising they deserve. If you find yourself wasting a fortune on pointless but creative advertising, don't blame your advertising agency. You commissioned them and you approved the garbage. So how do you avoid disaster?

To make the most of advertising and to direct your agency, you need a very clear advertising strategy. The good news is that this should be very short. The bad news is that it is far harder to be brief than long winded: being brief forces clear thinking and clear decisions.

An advertising strategy needs three short statements:

1 Benefit: What is the promise to our customers? What benefit or value will they gain from our service?

2 Reason why: Why should they believe that we can deliver on our promise?

3 Character: What is the character of our brand/product?

Table 9.2 illustrates how we can imagine the strategies for three detergents.

Here is why these strategies work:

- They focus on different types of customer: Fairy will work for new parents; Ariel might appeal more to parents with kids who go out and get dirty playing; Daz works for people who have plenty of white shirts which need to look smart.

- They are well differentiated: it would be hard to swap Ariel and Fairy. Ariel cannot claim to be really tough on stains and really gentle and mild. They are different ideas.

Table 9.2   Benefit, reason why, character

	Ariel	**Daz**	**Fairy**
Benefit	Removes toughest stains.	Keeps white clothes whiter.	Mild and safe.
Reason why	Biological formula.	It has a special blue whitener.	No harmful stuff in it.
Character	Scientific, advanced, reliable.	Cheap, cheery and friendly.	Caring.

- They work at the level of features, benefits, hopes and dreams. The features correspond roughly to the 'reason why' statement; the benefits statement explains itself; the character statement is the chance to explore hopes and dreams.
- They are all very simple, which forces clarity in advertising and communication.
- They give you a very clear brief against which to judge the relevance of any advertising ideas which are presented to you.

Achieving this level of simplicity and clarity is remarkably hard. But it is an investment which is well worth making: it will sharpen your advertising and marketing.

The advertising brief is your gateway to a sensible discussion with your advertising agency about both advertising and branding. When you have a clear brief about what the brand and the advertising are meant to achieve, then you can have a rational discussion about what works and what does not. Without a clear brief, you enter the realm of personal opinion, which simply leads to empty debate.

Clients get the advertising they deserve.

FURTHER READING

Books

Baylis, Nick (2005) *Learning from Wonderful Lives*, Wellbeing Press, Cambridge

Bennis, Warren (1989) *On Becoming a Leader*, Addison-Wesley, Reading, MA

Briggs Myers, Isabel (1995) *Gifts Differing: Understanding Personality Type*, Davies-Black, Mountain View, CA

Carnegie, Dale (1994) *How to Win Friends and Influence People*, Hutchinson, London

Collins, Jim (2001) *Good to Great*, Random House Business Books, London

Covey, Stephen R (1992) *The Seven Habits of Highly Effective People*, Simon & Schuster, London

Hesselbein, Frances and Cohen, Paul M (eds) (1999) *Leader to Leader*, Jossey-Bass, San Francisco, CA

Holmes, Andrew and Wilson, Dan (2004) *Pains in the Office*, Capstone, Oxford

Huppert, Felicia A, Baylis, Nick and Keverne, Barry (2005) *The Science of Well-being*, Oxford University Press, Oxford

Johnson, Spencer (1999) *Who Moved My Cheese?*, Vermilion, London

Kotter, John (1988) *The Leadership Factor*, Free Press, New York

Landsberg, Max (2000) *The Tools of Leadership*, HarperCollins, London

Lees, John (2004) *How to Get a Job You'll Love*, McGraw-Hill, Maidenhead

Machiavelli, Niccolò (1961) *The Prince*, Penguin Books, London

Minto, Barbara (2005) *The Pyramid Principle*, Financial Times Prentice Hall, London

Nelson, Bob (2005) *1001 Ways to Reward Employees*, Workman, New York

Nelson Bolles, Richard (2004) *What Color Is Your Parachute?*, Ten Speed Press, Berkeley, CA

Owen, Jo (2005) *How to Lead*, Prentice Hall, Harlow

Owen, Jo (2006) *Management Stripped Bare*, 2nd edn, Kogan Page, London

Peters, Thomas J and Waterman, Jr, Robert H (1982) *In Search of*

Excellence, Harper & Row, New York

Senge, Peter (1992) *The Fifth Discipline*, Random House, London

Sun Tzu (2003) *The Art of War*, Running Press Miniature Editions, Philadelphia, PA

Timpson, John (2002) *How to Be a Great Boss: The Timpson Way*, Timpson Ltd, Manchester

Wiseman, Richard (2003) *The Luck Factor*, Arrow Books, London

Harvard Business Review

Cialdini, Robert (2001) Harnessing the science of persuasion, HBR OnPoint Collection

Gabarro, John J and Kotter, John P (1993) Managing your boss, May–June

Goleman, Daniel (1998) What makes an effective leader, November–December

Goleman, Daniel (2000) Leadership that gets results, March–April

Kotter, John (1999) What effective general managers really do, March

Zaleznik, Abraham, Mintzberg, Henry and Gosling, Jonathan (2003) Your best managers lead and manage, HBR OnPoint Collection

Websites

Count Kostov (use and abuse of numbers): www.countkostov.blogspot.com

Desert exercise: www.wilderdom.com/games/descriptions/Survival Scenarios.html

Keirsey (good detail on MBTI): http://www.keirsey.com

Myers–Briggs: http://www.myersbriggs.org

Nick Baylis (excellent on personal wellbeing): http://www.nickbaylis.com

Self-testing psychometrics (free tests): www.similarminds.com

Self-testing psychometrics (part of British Psychological Society): www.psychtesting.org.uk

A fun site for personality analysis: www.colorquiz.com

INDEX

vision
creating for the organization 268–70
creating for the team 267–68
visualization, working to win 25–26

weaknesses
dealing with 23–24, 25
working round 158
white spaces 277
winning, principles of working to
win 25–26

work, changed nature of 19–20
work–life balance 51–53
working for yourself 38
working to win 25–26
writing skills 133–35

Xerox 277

yourself, understanding 59–61

Also available from **Jo Owen**

Myths of Leadership
Banish the Misconceptions and Become a Great Leader

9780749480745

Publishing October 2017

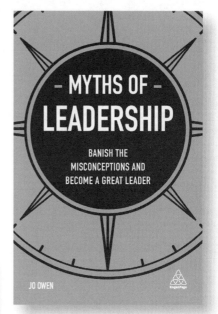

The Mindset of Success
Accelerate Your Career from Good Manager to Great Leader

9780749480356

Publishing December 2017